"Paul's book is an excellent treatment of a critical subject for I.S. executives across all industries. When you get right down to it, the success of any I.S. organization depends on service. It is the most important factor in building and maintaining the trust and confidence of the business. Paul's selection of topics and content, combined with his easy to understand writing style make this book a must have for all I.S. executives."

Ron J. Ponder
Chief Information Officer
AT&T

"I would characterize this book as essential reading for any I.S. manager who plans to stay employed through the '90s. I found the book to be a primer on the concept and implementation of a service organization. It is well organized, easy to read, and full of examples which drive home the key points. The various instruments and exercises contained within the book give it an interactive flavor that made me feel like I was participating in a seminar discussion."

George L. Frantz
Manager, Information Technology
ARCO Products Company

"I believe strongly that our ability to present I.S. as a service organization to our clients is critical to providing high value support to the business and will ensure long-term success. The key messages are also very consistent with Paul's previous writings on marketing the I.S. organization."

Jeff Carlson
Vice President, I.S.
Century Life of America

"Paul's vision that service be managed and permeate every aspect of what an I.S. organization does is now a bottom-line concern of every I.S. executive. Either you provide excellent information and technology services or become a 'business opportunity' for an outsourcing or systems integration company."

Dr. Donald A. Marchand
Dean & Professor
Syracuse University

"The transition from a technology focus to a service orientation will be the challenge for all I.S. professionals. Paul's book is based on many years of solid experience and provides the fundamentals necessary to guide us in realizing improved client service and satisfaction."

John Tremse
Sr. Vice President
Miles Inc.

"Paul has once again produced a no nonsense reminder for all I.S. professionals that our primary objective must be to deliver that most difficult by mandatory product-excellent client service."

John Ogrizovich
Vice President
Lone Star Gas Company

"I think the lessons learned here are most valuable. I see it as a must have, survival book in addition to being an excellent primer for the basics."

Nancy Robb
Harvard Community Health Plan

"Relevant, interesting. I was encouraged to think through my own situation."

Sean Baker
I.S. Client Services Manager
Dow Europe S.A.

"In today's competitive and strong client involvement culture, a world-class IM organization must be service-driven. Paul's book is not only informational and on target, but provides the tools, exercises, and direction for meeting this objective."

Patricia Wallington
Chief Information Officer
Xerox Corporation

"I found the book to be very worthwhile reading. Several times I found myself saying, 'Yeah, I knew that' about points that Paul articulated. However, I had never stopped to articulate them myself."

W. Ben Kuenemann
Senior Managing Director
Bear Stearns

"Credibility must be at the foundation of your relationship with your clients. If there were no clients, we wouldn't be needed."

James Venglarik
Director, Sales & Marketing
Glaxo, Inc.

"The information provided was very stimulating. I particularly enjoyed the chance to pause at the end of each chapter to reflect upon my own thoughts."

Chris Corbett
Business Systems Specialist
Dow Europe S.A.

I.S. AT YOUR SERVICE

I.S. AT YOUR SERVICE

Knowing and Keeping Your Clients

L. Paul Ouellette

KENDALL/HUNT PUBLISHING COMPANY
2460 Kerper Boulevard P.O: Box 539 Dubuque, Iowa 52004-0539

Contents

Acknowledgments

To Elaine, my wife and best friend for over thirty years. Her undying support and advice has truly benefitted this work and has always been important to me.

To my son John and his wife Carrie, professional writers in their own right who provide me with effective feedback.

To my daughter Denise and her husband Dan whose advice I cherish.

To Dan Roberts, president of O&A. Although extremely busy with daily managerial duties, always found the time to add value to this work.

To the following industry leaders who have taken their valuable time to read, edit, and submit value-added suggestions which enhanced this book's quality: Sean Baker, *Dow Europe*; Jeff Carlson, *Century Companies*; Raymond Ciarvella, *Data Tech*; Chris Corbett, *Dow Europe*; George Frantz, *ARCO Products Company*; Max Hopper, *American Airlines*; Dennis Jones, *Federal Express*; W. Ben Kuenemann, *Bear Stearns*; John Loewenberg, *Aetna*; Dr. Donald Marchand, *Syracuse University School of Information Studies*; John Ogrizovich, *Lone Star Gas*; John Owens, *Carrier Corporation*; Ron Ponder, *AT&T*; Dennis Popper, *NCR*; Danny Risener, *Publix Super Markets*; Nancy Robb, *Harvard Community Health Plan*; Jim Schultz, *Interprovincial Pipe Line*, Michael Simmons, *Bank of Boston*; John Tremse, *Miles Inc.*; James Venglarik, *Glaxo, Inc.*; Pat Wallington, *Xerox Corporation*

To Laurie Nicewicz, O&A's office administrator who has a joyful, service-oriented attitude that inspires us all.

With great appreciation, I thank Jill Vitiello and Ted Buswick for their contributions to this work.

To God, my higher power who has blessed me so dearly.

Introduction

In my travels I am frequently asked, "Where is the best strategic position for I.S.?" When will we (I.S.) receive the recognition at the corporate level?

We are aligned with our corporate goal but it doesn't seem to be enough. All around us we see re-positioning of I.S.—consolidation, rightsizing, outsourcing, competition, great client choices, etc. How do we gain recognition and keep a seat on the executive council?

Although I agree that these are turbulent times for our profession, we are also facing great opportunities. I.S. has finally left the back room and is fast moving into the mainstream of the business. Our technology as never before, is totally immersed into every aspect of our corporations. Our technology is the fiber by which our corporations function and are tied together. We have become a corporate asset beyond our focus on technology.

We live in an information-based society and we are the professionals who link it all together. It's a new playing field and most of us have never played in this corporate arena before.

We often lack the (soft) skills that are mandatory for long-term survival here. We need to create an awareness corporate-wide of our true, as opposed to our perceived value. We need to change our internal culture to be more responsive and service oriented. We need to operate as a cross-functional team.

As stated in the title, I strongly believe that developing a truly service-oriented I.S. organization is what will not only help us survive, but help position us for success well beyond the '90s.

Chapter 1

A Service Organization

"If we open a quarell between the past and the present, we shall find we have lost the future."

—*Winston Churchill*

At the Heart of I.S.

The work of the Information Processing Professional (IPP) has been called a science, an engineering discipline, and even an art. Calling our work a "Science" can easily be defended because programming is a clear example of the scientific method. State the problem, observe and experiment, then produce your hypothesis (the code) and test it.

"Engineering" is an applied field, and our work is of no use unless it is applied. "Software engineering" is used because the phrase is accurate; it's not used just to dignify the new kid on the scientific block.

Many of us within the I.S. profession view our work as "art." While the term "Black box" is often used negatively by people who don't understand what we do, it's certainly a creative label and usually requires solitary hours. It's also a talent that leaves many who are less skilled in our artistry in awe.

We can justify any of the three terms: Science, Engineering or Art. But would you categorize your work as "Service"? Service is probably not a term that quickly comes to mind, but that's what our function has become. Clients of the IPP are involved with computers more than they've ever been before, and have more knowledge about our work. Our organizations are moving in new directions, with a greater emphasis on networking and integration. In many cases we're competing with outside firms. These business facts combine to tell us that if we want to grow, or even maintain existing relationships with our clients, then we better provide good service.

In today's world of rightsizing, outsourcing, flatter hierarchies, and a competitive environment, service is more relevant than ever before. It is our saving grace, our caveat, our competitive edge toward being the information technology service provider of first choice.

Improving Your Skills

My purpose in this book is to bring the value of service to I.S. and improve your skills in three areas. When you finish, you should:

1. Understand the value that good service brings
2. Be able to identify where your service problems are, and
3. Know how to serve in and help build a service organization.

There are several ways to read this book. The best, speaking pedagogically, is to quickly read the whole book, getting the main ideas. Then go back and think about questions that are asked. Relate ideas to your own work, in detail. Fill in the Personal Action Plan Worksheets that follow each chapter. If you don't believe you have the time for that approach, then, as you do your single reading, please stop to answer questions that I raise while you're reading. And fill in the Worksheets.

I approach topics in what seems to me to be a natural order, first, in Section One, looking at the situation we're all in and setting a framework for improvements, then, in Section Two, working on skills to implement changes. Chapter 9, "Developing Your Service Strategy," is the one chapter with a narrower audience, since my advice applies primarily to managers. If that's not you, you can skip from the end of Chapter 8 straight to Chapter 10.

As you're reading, it may be a good idea to circle or make notes in the margin when I say something that applies specifically to you or your I.S. department. It not only will make it easier to review the ideas and your needs, but also it'll be interesting to compare your comments with others in your I.S. group who also read the book. Is your perception the same as that of your colleagues? Comparing what you've marked is one way to find out.

Over a long period of time I have seen most of the changes and business trends and how they've applied to computers. In my 33 years in I.S., I've been a senior executive in two large corporations and I've founded three service corporations. I've seen that most IPPs are strong technically, but need advice and training on the softer, people skills. Therefore, each of my companies was created to help the technical world adjust to the renewed interest in the human side of technology. Since I began Ouellette & Associates nine years ago to serve the I.S. community, over 1,000 companies have benefitted from our teaching and consulting.

A Blend: Total Quality and Service

Back in the '60s, the business trend was to do more, to have greater productivity. In the '70s, the emphasis was on doing things cheaper. The '80s taught us to do our work better. Now in the '90s we're hearing how we can do everything quicker. More often than not, the technique that blends "more," "cheaper," "better," and "quicker" is often thought as Total Quality Management, or whatever comparable phrase your company has chosen in its attempt to be distinctive. Note: I am well aware that many TQM initiatives are seriously considered effective and very successful and I fully support these initiatives.

Improving I.S. service is a part of the well heralded Total Quality movement, but don't think of the two as the same. Total Quality is often defined as giving the customer everything he needs, and more. First this idea hit manufacturing. That was where it was easiest to apply. Everyone understands quality on an assembly line. Everyone knows about inspection, about the percentage of faulty parts shipped. But it was new, to some, to think about correcting the problem before the part ever reaches manufacturing, to think about working with people in another department to stop problems before they become visible.

Many positive changes have grown from the Quality movement. One, used in product development, is concurrent or simultaneous engineering. When a new product is being planned, the process should no longer be that:

- First, planning thinks of it
- Then, the designer designs it
- Then, assembly makes it
- Then, marketing decides how to market it
- Then, packaging decides how to ship it
- Then, sales sells it
- And then customers figure out if they can use it.

Now the plan is for everyone to work together from the outset. Let's be sure the design, when executed, will be easy to assemble. Let marketing say if the product has the right features or services, have your customers participate in the plans whenever possible. Make long range plans to work with specific vendors and have them contribute their expertise as part of the team, rather than just looking for the lowest cost. As you read these "new" ideas, you're probably considering if and how you're already applying them in I.S.

Total Quality is a movement that's making businesses respond the way they should have been all along. Service is a key, grassroots part of Total Quality. Total Quality is a movement; service has to be a habit. Total Quality programs can be unwieldy; service is a series of controllable moments.

Serving the I.S. Client

As the concern for Quality shifted beyond the product line to the administrative and support areas of the company, people in sales, administration, and I.S. began to see themselves as producing products. They began to see the chain of events that led to them and from them. They began to evaluate the necessity for each step in that chain, how those steps could be changed for greater efficiency, and how to provide the best service for those who receive their products. In our case, the people along that chain are our clients.

Maybe I should pause a minute to explain the term I use most often, clients and why I feel strongly that it's the proper way to refer to the people we serve. When I ask IPPs in my seminars how they refer to those they serve, I hear terms such as users, customers and clients. To me a "user" or "end-user" is just what is implied. It's someone who uses a product or service. There's no relationship being built; they are just the ones dangling at the end of the line, using what we produce. Most of the time, we'll never even see them. Although this is workable and does produce results, it's pretty much a hit-and-run situation and not in the best interest of building long-term relationships.

Typically a "customer" is someone who comes to us, we fill a need, and they leave. There's typically no relationship beyond the immediate. We do our best to help them, here and now, then forget them and go on to the next customer. The customers may come back or may not, and if they do it doesn't matter who provides the service. This is certainly a step up from "end user" and is appropriate to use, but still does not connect us in a shared responsibility status nor does it imply an effort towards a longer term relationship.

The term "client", in my opinion, strongly implies a shared responsibility. My client and I are on the same level as we work towards an understanding of the service expectations. His or her problem becomes my problem. I strive to build a relationship on a foundation of trust, respect, and understanding of each others' position. It is built on the premise that it will be a reoccurring relationship.

At one recent seminar, a woman said that she considers clients to be external, while those who come for assistance internally are treated as members of the same team. She realized that internal people did not receive the same respect or speed of service as external people, but they should. Everyone you serve, internal or external, I believe, is equally your client.

What Is Service?

I feel that one problem we have had with client relationships stems from a basic misunderstanding of what "service" means. In these opening chapters, we'll work together toward a definition. Before we begin, take a look at the service your I.S. group provides. What is it? Take a moment and think of a definition of service that suits you.

Don't search for the perfect definition; take the first one that comes to you—that's probably what you really think—and write it down.

What did you come up with? Based on responses in my seminars, here are some of your choices:

- Keeping clients happy
- Providing what clients need
- Filling client needs "as quickly as I can"
- Serving the company's computer needs
- Giving clients everything they want when they want it

We have to ask ourselves, "If we are truly a service organization, does that mean that the client is always right?"

Put that last question in the perspective of your own experiences. Think of a couple of times that the client appeared to have been wrong. In these instances, why was the client wrong? Was it fully the client's fault? Were there any acts of commission or omission by I.S. that contributed to the problem? Is anyone really "wrong"?

Quite likely, at least one of your examples has a client with unrealistic demands. If you don't give clients everything they say they need, what are they going to do—go elsewhere for service? In the past, no, but in the present, quite possibly. But what if the client's request doesn't fit your corporate direction or your standard software or your established procedures? And how do you balance the large-scale, longer-range corporate direction needs with the multitude of short-range requests from clients?

It's clear that we can't give clients everything they want. We can't do everything at once. We need priorities. We have to influence our clients so they believe that going with us is the right way for them to go. How successful have we been in influencing them? Well, history indicates to me that we haven't been very effective in building the relationship needed for influence to work. The trust factor which results from a strong relationship isn't usually where we need it to be.

The Waiter

Let's take an example to think a bit more about service. I'd like you to imagine yourself in this scenario. You're out for a dinner in a classy restaurant with your significant other. You're sitting there romantically gazing into each other's eyes. You've been sitting for ten minutes and nobody's offered you any service. So you stop a waiter walking by and ask for service. He says, "Sorry, but it's not my table," and walks into the kitchen. What would you do?

You might leave, or maybe tell the manager, or sit there and stew a bit over the lousy service. The guy was rude to you, wasn't he? But wait a minute. What did the waiter do wrong? He was brought up on Captain Kangaroo and always acts as a good Do-Bee. He always tells the truth, and it's not his table. It really isn't. He was just being honest with you, so what right do you have to be upset? He could lose his job if you complain to the manager, and all because he told you the truth.

Now think, what's the real reason you're upset?

Probably it was because he didn't meet your expectations. Now we're getting closer to a real definition of service. You had a certain level of expectation and he didn't match up to it. And whether you talk to the manager or walk out, you'll probably complain to friends about the lousy service you got at that restaurant.

What if the waiter had said to you, "We're shorthanded today because Bob, Sue and Joan called in sick." Would that have helped? It might soften your anger a bit, but do you really care? No. Should you? No, of course not. What if your meal arrived late, and when it was delivered, you were told, "We're sorry for the delay, but the chef was taken ill and we're filling in back there as well as we can." Would that have been satisfactory to you? I doubt it. You may feel sympathetic, but it wouldn't lead you to come back. You're paying for good service and you're not getting it, and that's the bottom line. You have expectations, and they're not being met.

Would everyone think the same way as you do about this situation? Certainly not. Everyone's expectations are different. However, there are some basic principles to follow in providing excellent service.

Personal Service

Now let's turn it back to your situation. What do you think goes through your client's mind when an I.S. person says, "Oh, I'd like to help you, but it's not my application." Or "Sara takes care of that, not me." Your client sees fingers pointing in all directions and feels she's not getting good service.

How should the waiter have handled your initial request for service, and how should you handle a legitimate request that's not in your area? The waiter's attitude is contrary to good service. First, it would be much more helpful for the waiter to say, "I'll speak to your waiter," or, similarly, for you to say, "That's Sara's responsibility. I'll see if she's available."

What if you take the client to Sara? If she's in the same area you can walk your client over. What message are you sending then? Or if she's not in the area, pick up the phone and tell the client, "Let me call her for you and see if she's there." These actions are not very time-consuming for you, and your client has a much better feeling about you and your organization. You've given the client the message that you care and have taken a first step in meeting her/his service expectation.

100% Satisfaction

Service is not giving everything to everybody the moment they want it. No one can realistically meet those expectations. But an expectation for *how* you provide service to a person can be met every time. Can you get 100% satisfaction from all your clients? You're probably thinking, "Of course not. That's pie in the sky. Unrealistic." I disagree. I'm going to challenge that thinking. You *can* get 100% satisfaction from everyone.

You may not be able to act immediately on the client's needs and full expectations, but you can have every client leave every transaction feeling good about what went on, saying, "I didn't receive my total requirements, but I really like working with these folks." Service is more of an attitude of how we interact with others than a driving concern for meeting a budget or keeping priorities perfectly in line. And those "others" even include people in your own department.

We in I.S. sometimes have problems agreeing with each other. We're such a diverse group, coming from segments of expertise: tech support, applications, database administration, telecommunications, operations, etc. Even within I.S., we don't always understand each other's worlds. We need to give the same level of courtesy and service to internal clients, external clients, and our co-workers within I.S.

Service is not a goal; it's a process to be believed and lived. The goal is to be computer supplier of first choice. And we can make it happen!

The Changed Climate

Clients know a lot more about our business than they used to. The mystery of the computer is gone. The days of the guru in the clean computer room are mostly gone. The coming of the personal computer allowed everyone in the organization with technical leanings to think of himself as a "computer person," not necessarily someone with great computer skills, but at least someone with a basic understanding.

Remember the early days of PCs when unauthorized PCs began to appear? Next, supposed expertise began to spurt up around the organization. Rarely was this sanctioned by us, and in many cases, we decided to look the other way. Magazines and books on "personal computing" poured from the publishers until consumers were glutted with the learning possibilities. And all this brought much of our formerly specialized knowledge into the realm of everyman.

> *We can be the provider of choice every time we want to be. All we have to do is rightly deserve to be that choice.*

A common I.S. view at the time was to clamp down. "We" control computers. "We" will not have any upstart, unauthorized PCs in our domain. Admittedly, much in our viewpoint was easily justified. Our software and hardware forced us to be regimented. Our problem was in our approach, attempting to be authoritarian. We weren't convincing our clients and potential clients of why we should be their computer services provider of choice. We were telling them that we had to be. Such an approach is bound to stir rebellion, and it certainly did.

Does this recent history ring true to you? Some IPPs may look at these occurrences as the beginning of the end, as the first steps in the decentralization of computers. But if you share a mutual respect and trust with your clients, that's not the case. We now know that we have to deserve their trust, and we earn trust through outstanding service. We can be the provider of choice every time we want to be. All we have to do is rightly deserve to be that choice.

Time for Reflection

Let's pause for an exercise on identifying "service". Take a few minutes to develop answers to the following questions. Then compare your answers with mine, not to have a right or wrong answer but simply improving our understanding of service.

1. What is service within I.S.?
2. What is the basic element of service? Put a number of these elements together and we have the full service picture.
3. What is your worst service story, and what made service so bad?
4. What is your best service story, and what made service so good?

Here are my answers.

1. What is service within I.S.? It's being prompt, being courteous, understanding what the client wants, being professional. Think of a place that consistently maintains that kind of service. DisneyLand or Disney World are often cited as examples of excellent service. Everyone you meet is going to be neat, clean and courteous. Whether a sweeper on the sidewalk or someone behind a counter—everyone acts professionally and provides top service. That's no accident. It's a matter of an attitude and a process. Maybe IPPs need a professional Disney-like attitude. The goal of service is to manage expectations so as to provide customer satisfaction at or beyond the customer's expectations.
2. What is the basic element of service? It's a microorganism. It's a small point. Everything can be going smoothly and one word, one gesture can turn it all around to bad service. But there are ways to plan for and properly handle all these tiny

moments when service is provided. I'll say much more about these moments of service later.

3. Have you recalled several unfortunate service stories? Let's take a closer look at how a tiny moment or statement can affect the client's perspective of the quality of service. I'll use a few true service stories to illustrate.

I was flying first class on a major airline and after a good meal (considering I was eating airline food) I asked the flight attendant if I could have more coffee. She instantly replied, "Let me finish picking up the glasses and then I'll be glad to get it for you." Now on the surface this seems OK, but it didn't make me feel "first class." It really made me feel second class to the dishes. Although it was phrased politely, the message I got was, "Settle back, buddy, and I'll serve your coffee when I get around to it."

Another story involves an incident with a hotel front desk. Upon checking in, I realized I didn't receive the room I'd requested and been told I'd have. I said, "I was told I'd have a non-smoking room." The clerk said, "I'm sorry, sir, but the non-smoking rooms go first, and they're all taken." I said, "If I need to guarantee the room with you, why can't you guarantee the room I'll receive?" A question like that usually gets me a look like, "Are you crazy, mister?" But it's a good question. Why should the customer be the one making the guarantees? She proceeded to read me the policy and how she can't control these situations and how she was truly sorry but that's how the cookie crumbles. Escalating to higher management produced, "We only have so many non-smoking rooms and if I held one aside for you someone else would be mad." For some reason, that statement did not quite relieve my concerns. I finally asked, "Could you please spray the room for freshness?" The immediate response was, "The maintenance crew is gone for the day and we don't do that." Knowing at this point that this would be a no-win situation and recognizing the late hour, I stayed but never to return.

Look at your worst service story. What could have been done to turn the horror story into a successful service story? What were the key moments where a change in action, word or gesture would have made a tremendous difference?

4. To illustrate how good service can be achieved, let's look at a few positive stories. You can probably fit yours right in with my list. One of the best I've heard comes from a major department store chain that extends into Alaska. Its Alaska store is the only one that sells tires. Well, someone bought tires at the store in Alaska, then later moved down to the lower 48, to the East Coast in fact, and (you can see it coming) the customer had trouble with the tires so he brought them into a local branch of the same store.

How do you picture most sales people responding? Probably much like the waiter, with an "I'm sorry, but we don't deal in tires. You'll have to contact the store where you purchased them." But not this salesperson. The employee took back the tires and shipped them to Alaska. She took full ownership of the problem and all the responsibility for seeing that the tire problem was resolved, and the result was a happy customer—a happy customer who will continue to shop at and talk positively about that store, wherever he lives.

This department store salesperson saw herself as a part of the whole. In manufacturing today, there's an emphasis being put on understanding how your job fits into the entire process, on seeing yourself as one important cog in the larger wheel. The whole wheel depends on you doing your job right, and you're given the authority to see that your job is done right. Like many things that fall under the Total Quality banner, this attitude first became prominent in manufacturing, but today it applies to all jobs, I.S. as much as any other.

I have one more department store story. An out-of-town customer who was not familiar with the area was making a purchase, and while doing so was explaining to the clerk how she needed to get to the airport. The clerk said that it was very close, and began explaining the turns. After realizing that this was confusing, the clerk said, "Look, I have a little time. Let me take you there." The clerk got someone else to take his counter and drove the visitor to the airport.

Now I realize this case is exceptional. Most people can't actually drop their work to help someone. But it did happen, and it happened because the clerk was attuned to helping others. The point to both of these success stories is that the salespeople went outside of their "boxes" to provide service. They had the right attitudes, and they had the authority to do the right thing. You can bet that their actions won't be forgotten. The customers will not only remember that store, but will tell others about that outstanding service, too.

Since I told a poor service hotel story, let me add a positive one. I arrived at the McCormick Center Hotel in Chicago for a conference I was speaking at. As soon as the clerk heard my name, I was asked if I could wait just a moment. I said, "Sure," and wondered why. Several people gathered together behind the front desk and began singing, "Congratulations, your book has been accepted by a publisher." They took a straightforward message from my office and got creative about delivering it! Such a thoughtful and creative message has long stuck in my mind as an example of how to be creative with good service—and have some fun, too.

Perceptions of IPPs

All too often, the I.S. person is thought of as a stereotype. Some of the most commonly perceived traits include being:

- Intelligent
- Analytical
- Quiet
- Introspective
- White
- Male

and wearing a nerd pack in his shirt pocket. He may think of his family as valued peripherals. Think of your department. How true is that stereotype? How true was it five years ago? Ten years ago? Most likely it was more true then than now. But there is a basis in the past for this stereotype. And even today, most of us do prefer technology to people.

A few years ago I read a survey conducted to determine the predominant personality traits of IPPs (while I remember the fundamentals of the survey, I haven't been able to track down the source). The results show us where the stereotype comes from. What do you think is our #1 trait? According to the study, #1 is being introverted. No, this doesn't mean we are nerds. As a population, we enjoy time alone.

We enjoy working by ourselves. This doesn't mean that we don't function well with other people; it just says what we prefer. Does that fit you? Trait #2 is that, as a group, we tend to be musically inclined. That seems to follow from our logical view, flow and orderliness of things.

Trait #3 is that we're self-starting. That trait comes in handy when we're also introverted. We don't require external motivation. Since we're self-starters, we may not immediately recognize that many, many people need outside motivation. Being self-starters may make us initially suspicious of working in teams, because we're eager to start working and may see all the collaboration as unnecessary, or as slowing us down.

Whether you see it as fair or unfair the I.S. people are often viewed as a type. Too often, another characteristic of that "type" is "unresponsive." How often, out of our hearing, do our clients complain about how long it takes for us to complete a project? How often do requests for I.S. projects never even get made because such a long delay is expected? Or because the I.S. department is not easy to deal with? Do we have any mechanism for even knowing the answers to these questions?

The Need to Educate

It's true that developing new applications takes time—sometimes a great deal of time. Therefore, our clients may be right in their assessment of the amount of time something takes us. We shouldn't fault them for what they don't know about our work. There's no reason why they should know the tortures caused by incompatible protocols or equipment, or the headaches brought on by modifying existing applications.

If we're losing business or creating unhappy clients because they don't fully understand what we do and how we can help them, it may be largely our own fault. We need to educate them, and to manage their expectations. Right now, do your clients come to you with ideas that are impossible (or at least improbable) to execute, or with timetables that challenge the speed of light? Well, have IPPs ever made a concerted effort to educate their ignorance away, to train people in how we in I.S. can make a difference in their work? Much of that education involves better marketing of our services, which is beyond the scope of this book, but is covered in a previous book of mine, *How to Market the I/S Department Internally* (AMACOM, 1991).

After you finish a project, how much training do you provide for clients? You need to educate them. Coach them to understand how technology can serve them best, rather than being a thorn in their sides. Show them how just two days of training may save weeks of work over the course of a year.

PCs have actually helped to bring us all closer together, as peers. More and more people in the company now use our services. Every department needs us. This is a new era of working together, but we in I.S. have to take the initiative!

Stepping Into Prominence

We all know that the gurus and consultants have been preaching changes, but for most people there really hasn't been a major change. When it comes to our daily client approaches to doing business we have moved forward in leaps and bounds when it comes to technology, but daily client business-interaction? In fact, I would venture a guess that some of you may see this service-orientation as just another fad.

This is a mistake. If you approach service as another fad, then that's what it will be in your organization. But the rest of the world will leave you behind. Attention to service is required in today's business. And if you're not yet focussing on service inside your I.S. department, you haven't yet tuned in to the necessities of doing business in the 1990s. Unlike some of the past fads such as having gurus preach to you, "We need and must form partnerships with our clients," what does forming partnerships really mean? Does my client base want or have the same understanding of partnering? And most importantly, how do I accomplish a successful partnership (a little more on this later). This book will provide you with not only answers to your questions relative to forming a successful service-oriented I.S. organization but the how as well.

I.S. should be an admired group, but not admired from afar as before. Now the admiration should be based on the fact that we're helpful, because we're easy to work with, because we always approach a problem in the same constructive manner, and because we've learned how to manage expectations. Isolation for techies is gone. IPPs have emerged from the back room to take a prominent seat in corporate America. And that's right where we should be.

Personal Action Plan

The lasting value of this book lies in the behavior and thought changes that you bring back to the job. To make that transfer easier, we provide the skeletal framework for your Personal Action Plan. At the end of each chapter will be a worksheet where you can make notes in two areas: specific ideas that may be used on your job, and specific actions you'd like to take within thirty days.

At the end of the book there will be a process for bringing the Personal Action Plan notes together into a more cohesive plan.

PERSONAL ACTION PLAN

Worksheet

A SERVICE ORGANIZATION

Specific ideas I can use on the job:

Example:

—Start working on influencing my clients rather than being dictatorial.

—I will start personalizing my services. (Add your own.)

Specific actions I will take within 30 days:

—Start a technology initialization educational project geared solely towards my clients.

—Work at generating a service-oriented attitude. Work hard at truly understanding what service means.

Chapter 2

Treat Your Clients with Respect

"There's no one grand stroke that does it. It's a lot of little steps."
—Peter A. Cohen

Meeting the Computer Industry Challenge

I recently attended a sales meeting of a computer manufacturer. The vice president of sales got up in front and told all the reps in the audience:

> Here's how we're gonna sell our hardware and software services this year. We'll go directly to the client community, not to I.S., but to the users, the clients that I.S. supports. We'll convince them that if they buy from us, they'll need minimal interaction with their I.S. groups.

That approach is happening a great deal. Look at where software technology is going today. Software houses are writing software much more for the client than for the I.S. community. And the software is often run with a simple menu or by voice-driven commands. We're seeing more expert systems and neural systems designed for ease of use by the business client. The PCs that once seemed like toys are now often serving as workstations and are networked together.

We need to adjust to this changing situation. Our appropriate response is action, not fear or accusations. There's new competition that we have to be aware of, and we must monitor their activity to determine what competencies will be required of us so that we know we're at least as competent. We do have a built-in advantage. We're closer, more accessible. In most cases we're networked and know our company culture. But that may not be enough.

While the clients want software that helps them perform their functions, they don't necessarily want to be involved in operating systems, networking architecture, and peripherals. More than ever, they need our help determining hardware configurations and customizing their new software. To be effective at this, we must deserve their business by knowing how to service them for their current and changing needs.

> *When clients have the need, they want to turn to you as a service organization where they can be respected and have their needs addressed, where they'll be addressed as clients in a peer-to-peer situation.*

Should We Be Partners?

We should treat our clients with an eye toward the future of the relationship. We're all in this together for the long haul. Perhaps you've heard the word "partnering" tossed around over the past few years. Although this has benefits as a principle it is also in part, an example of a fad word, and at the first sign of a new bandwagon some managers will religiously hop aboard. Before they jumped, did they consider the questions, "What is partnering?" and "Do clients really want it?"

In my experience clients don't necessarily want you to be a partner. This advice may fly in the face of what you read, but first take a moment and decide what "partnership" means to you or may mean to your clients.

Your answers probably range from being fused at the hip (wherever my client goes I go), to understanding my client's business to the umpteenth level of detail, to simply knowing each other on a personal basis and being able to comfortably say, "Hi Joan," when you meet in the hall. Those are all forms of partnerships.

What clients often tell me is that they want a partnership that leads you to know *enough* about their business needs and main concerns so that you can address those needs through a possible technical solution when they come to you, and that you'll make them comfortable dealing with you. When they have the need, they want to turn to you as a service organization where they can be respected and have their needs addressed, where they'll be addressed as clients in a peer to peer situation.

So in its underlying, basic meaning, all partnership means is cooperation, looking for how different parties can work together to make things better for both of them. This is something that always needs to be done. Too often a new term is latched onto, but the depth of the underlying concept is not. Partnering is an exciting term today, but in the managerial scrapheap tomorrow. Long after "partnering" is gone, the need for cooperation and understanding remains.

Keeping Your Clients

It is estimated that attracting a new client costs five to six times more than maintaining an existing one. Therefore it's economical to try to satisfy your current clients. But perhaps the requests for I.S. services are so backed up that you don't think you have to worry about keeping clients, and don't have time to mess about with superior service, either. Well, think about this. If your service is poor, if you don't satisfy your clients, the clients are more likely to have problems with the work you've already done, and there goes your time into maintenance and after-the-fact training. That's less time providing up-front service, and your clients may well start looking elsewhere for service.

We must be the information technology service provider of choice. Price is not a leading weapon. Taking the low bid for a product or service is becoming less common. Bidding itself is less common because there are more long-term relationships going on so that suppliers don't have to bid for each new project.

Studies have shown that people are willing to pay for superior service. A study of general service organizations on "Why Customers Quit," conducted by the Technical Assistance Research Program in Washington, D.C. (TARP) shows that those with high client service saw a 6% increase in market share per year even though they charged 9% more for their services than companies without high client service. The TARP study will be referred to frequently in this chapter.

Keeping existing clients is not just a matter of treating those clients well. We have to respond uniformly to everyone. All IPPs must view the rest of the company as potential clients, and treat them accordingly.

Considering Your Clients' Options

How many of your clients do you think are, in some way, dissatisfied with I.S. work? 10%? 25%? 40%? How do you know if they're not pleased? Do they tell you? Probably not very many of them. "Why Customers Quit" shows that service organizations only hear from 4% of their dissatisfied clients. If you believe you get a lot of complaints, just imagine if they all spoke up. The other 96% will just walk away.

Put yourself in their shoes. How often do you complain about poor service? Most likely you follow the same procedure. If a salesperson in a store gives you poor service, you'll just go to the competitor next time. There's usually someone else to go to, and that's a lot easier to do.

Our clients used to have nowhere else to go to get the services we provide. But, as we can see in Figure 2-1, that's no longer the case. The New Competition includes a host of providers once considered our allies. Our clients can outsource to these new competitors, plus they're more likely to have someone in their department who wants

Figure 2-1. The New Competition

Professional Consultants
Software Vendors
Hardware Vendors
Department Computer Experts
Software Programs
User Groups

to try a solution. The economic hard times for many computer companies have created a surplus of consultants. Software vendors are more active with service. Desktop computers solve problems that used to be solved only by the gurus in the glass room. There are user groups based around different applications.

In my view, IPPs should be instrumental in establishing and running client user groups in your organization because these groups will help to educate your clients. The results of this education may not be what you expect. You may think that once clients better understand their applications and are able to solve some of their own problems, then they'll no longer come to you for minor adjustments and maintenance. To some extent that's true, but more knowledge breeds more questions. The questions will actually increase in number, but they'll be more intelligent, at a higher level.

The client user groups are valuable to you because they show your respect for clients by sharing knowledge with them. By giving them knowledge, you're giving them the authority to help themselves. Education helps establish realistic client expectations and build a better IPP/client relationship. Many organizations that I have worked with have had great success with this philosophy.

Through cooperation, understanding and sharing of knowledge, you're creating a team atmosphere. It's then comfortable to ask your client, "How are we doing? How can we do better?" And because they understand you better than they used to, you'll get useful answers. The more you read in this book, the more obvious it will be that consistently high client service provides an opportunity for tremendous payoffs.

Why Clients Defect

Let's get back to those 96% of clients dissatisfied with service who'll just walk away. I can hear you saying that these statistics are for service in general. They may apply to a typical store sales situation, "but I'm not going to have 96% of my dissatisfied clients walk away." You're right. They're linked to you by the organization. But think a moment. That link alone can cause resentment. That link can be seen as a restraint on free choice, and at your first service slip-up, the client may run to an external service provider.

Even if the I.S. defection rate is lower than in an average service organization, there's still cause for concern. The trend is pervasive enough; there's enough carryover to make this data useful for opening our IPP eyes. Of those clients who leave us and never return:

- 68% leave because of the service provider's bad attitude or indifference
- 14% are dissatisfied with the product or service
- 9% leave for competitive reasons
- 5% develop other relationships
- 3% move away.

The same survey indicates that, on the average, it takes twelve positive client service interactions to make up for one negative one. How much easier it is to simply avoid the negative. I know that it isn't easy to change the way things have been done for years. Strong effort is required by every IPP, as is the full support of senior management.

In I.S., I believe the percentage of clients leaving for competitive reasons is higher than 9%. Outsourcing is becoming common. And look who's getting into it—even IBM. When a computer giant comes to your door and says, "Thou shalt outsource!" what's the internal reaction going to be? "Well, these guys sure know their stuff; maybe we should consider it." This situation is reality. But we can successfully compete against it! I *know* we can!

The study also states that 5% will leave because of a personal relationship. As an example, think of why you prefer a particular bank. It may well be that you're comfortable dealing with one or two particular tellers. It may have nothing to do with the quality of the service, but just be a positive personal impression. We can't control outside relationships, but we can work to strengthen our own relationships.

Look at the 68% who may leave, not because of anything distinctly negative, but because there was nothing distinctly positive from the service provider. You may have worked for three months to solve a problem the client has, your solution may be satisfactory, yet the client doesn't think highly enough of you to come back. If your technical solution was right, then the human interaction may well be at fault.

Figure 2-2.

REPURCHASE INTENTION (TARP)

INDUSTRY	WITH PROBLEM	WITHOUT PROBLEM	CHANGE
Auto Parts/Service	70%	80%	10%
Health Care	75%	95%	20%
Insurance	50%	80%	30%
Office Equipment	**70%**	**90%**	**20%**
Retail Banking	40%	60%	20%

If there is a real problem with a product, how many clients will repurchase from the same source?

Roughly, one in five clients who have problems will not return. By eliminating problems you should save 20% of your clients. That's a sizeable chunk of your client base. In a company with 85,000 employees, 20% is 17,000 of them.

Even though that's a significant number of clients saved by eliminating problems, these statistics indicate that more people will leave you because of poor service than because of problems with your products. Eliminating product problems must be addressed, but not at the expense of improving service.

The Great Client Freeze-Out

If you only hear from 5% of those who are dissatisfied, what do the rest do? Do they just keep their mouths shut, or will they complain to a colleague at lunch, or during a coffee break, or when someone asks where to go to get a problem solved. Take a look at The Complaint Iceberg.

As you can see; the vast majority of complaints may or may not ever reach you. Although I can appreciate letting sleeping dogs lie, we need to know what is going on beneath the surface, or be totally at a loss, or at their mercy when they awake. I strongly suggest that we go out and research what is going on beneath the obvious. Then and only then can we effectively structure a successful strategy that will move us toward the goal and objective of being an involved, respected and viewed asset of our our corporation.

Figure 2-3.

The Complaint Iceberg

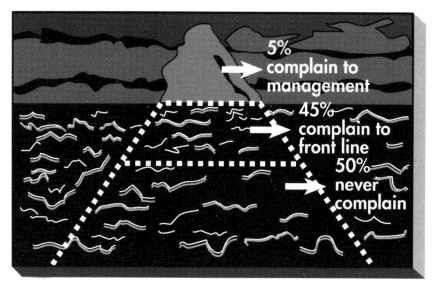

Source: Technical Assistance Research Programs. Presented at National Quality Forum IV, October 5, 1988.

The Formula

There's a very basic approach to satisfying clients, I apply a simple formula:

Do-it-right-the-first-time + Complaint Management = Satisfaction

In seminars, an IPP will usually speak up to say, "What's this 'first time' bit? Isn't the idea to do it right, period?" Sure it is, but doing it right should be accepted procedure without needing mention. Three years ago if you could "do it right," whether technical application or human interaction, then you were in the driver's seat.

Now, though, nearly everyone has improved their processes so that they're doing it right. The competitive advantage now is in doing it right "the first time." Pie in the sky, you say? Nay, say I. You *can* do it right the first time, every time. But you've got to realize that it's possible. That realization in the mind has to come before it's a reality in fact.

Here's an example. When you started college, what kinds of grades did you hope to achieve? 4.0? 3.5? That's what you hoped for, but what did you expect? Perhaps a 2.5? And what did you get? Mostly likely around a 2.5. You lived up to your expectations.

I'm telling you that you can have the right interaction with your client the first time, every time. And remember, doing it right isn't doing everything the client wants. It's treating the client the way the client expects to be treated, or better.

D.I.R.T.F.T.

I've often used an acronym in place of "Do-it-right-the-first-time," but some have thought it inappropriate—D.I.R.T.F.T. They say, "if the concept is positive, then why use an acronym that begins with 'DIRT'?" I come back with, "Because if you're going to do it right the first time, you have to get your hands dirty." You can't sit back passively, in isolation and work on the problem that's been given to you. You've got to jump into the trenches feet first, and understand the problem from the perspective of the person who'll be implementing your solution. That's the only way to be sure your solution will be appropriate.

"O.K., I can buy that," you say," but it's not an acronym you can pronounce. Acronyms only catch on if they're short enough so you can say the letters, like TV or CIA, or easy to pronounce, like NASA or laser." (Did you know that "laser" means *Light Amplification by Stimulated Emission of Radiation?*) Well, DIRTFT is hard to pronounce. But you're forgetting that "FT" is an abbreviation in itself. Therefore, DIRTFT is "DIRT FOOT," quite appropriate for working in the trenches.

So, DIRTFT + Complaint Management = Satisfaction

Complaint Management

Before leaving all those people who don't complain, let's see why they keep quiet (at least to us, if not about us). There are three key reasons:

- It's not worth the time and trouble
- No one will care about the problem
- There's no useful way to complain

There's a lot of overlap in these reasons. They show that often there's no system for complaint management in place.

Look again at The Complaint Iceberg. Because we don't naturally hear most of the complaints, we've got to encourage them. The idea is not to hang out our dirty linen; it's not to catch those doing things wrong. The idea is to improve, to look at the processes and figure out how something can be done better, to harness the complaints and ride 'em into the ground. By improving, we keep clients. If we promptly, properly handle complaints, statistics say that 80% of those with the complaints will buy again. Later in this book, when you're mapping out the steps you need to implement your service strategy, you'll again see that Complaint Management is essential. By effectively dealing with complaints, we can make a stronger client relationship than if we had never made a mistake.

A Quick Evaluation

Consider your own clients. At this point, you may well say, we conduct surveys regularly and our clients love us. I ask that you put that notion aside for now and consider how many of your clients are probably below the Iceberg's water line.

How do the dissatisfaction percentages for general service organizations given in the preceding pages compare? Write down your estimates and discuss them with others. Recognize that your clients are not likely to think as well of I.S. as I.S. does of itself. You're not perceived by others the same way you perceive yourself.

1. What percentage of I.S. complaints do you hear?
2. What percentage of your client base is well satisfied with your work?

3. If your I.S. clients have a problem, how many people will they tell? Will the number be different if it's a small or a large problem?
4. If your clients are pleased with your work, how many people will they tell?

A fact of human nature is that bad news will spread faster than good news. I'll turn to TARP once again for statistics on question 3. It is estimated that if someone has a small problem, involving a less than $50 expenditure, and it's handled well, that person will tell five people about their problem—even though they were satisfied. And then there's the ripple effect as the word gets passed on as third-hand information, quite possibly with facts changed as the story takes on a life of its own.

If people were dissatisfied with the resolution of a small problem, the number of people told doubles, ten people will get told. Think of the ripple effect there.

Now let's move to a larger problem, with over $100 involved. The problem is corrected to the individual's satisfaction, but it wasn't all smooth getting satisfaction. In such a case, TARP studies indicate that eight people will be told. If they're dissatisfied, sixteen will be told with a much greater on-going ripple effect.

Now think about your own relationships with your clients. How do those statistics fit in. How do they compare with the answers that you gave in question 3?

To finish this chapter on a positive note, if all the complaints you hear are addressed quickly, courteously, and effectively, what percentage of the complainers will come back to you with their future needs? Unless you have a captive audience without choice, 90% will return. Think of the positive effect that 90% will have on current or future I.S. clients? I don't know about you, but I'll go for the positive odds at every chance. The beauty is that to achieve this high percentage of returning clients, as this book will demonstrate, doesn't require massive changes to be able to perform at this level. Heck, we won't even have to consider what we are most known for, reorganization.

PERSONAL ACTION PLAN

Worksheet

TREAT YOUR CLIENTS WITH RESPECT

Specific ideas I can use on the job:

Specific actions I will take within 30 days:

Chapter 3

The Service Strategy Cycle

"Never take anything for granted."

—*Benjamin Disraeli*

The Client At the Center

After dealing with the issue of I.S. client service over a long period of time, we developed an approach to help bring this into perspective. We call it the Service Strategy Cycle. Let's take a look at the working components of the cycle, starting with the service philosophy which is at the top in Figure 3-1.

As you can see, in the center of the cycle is our client surrounded by all the elements that provide excellent service. Service Philosophy is at the top because all else springs from it. Do you have a service philosophy that everyone agrees with? Is it written down, or just an understood way of operating? If you don't have a written philosophy, you should consider it. To succeed, your service philosophy needs to be supported by your management. If it's not supported from the top, then other priorities are more likely to push service aside. Management support is critical if we're to obtain needed resources or cultivate a service attitude.

Figure 3-1. The Service Strategy Cycle

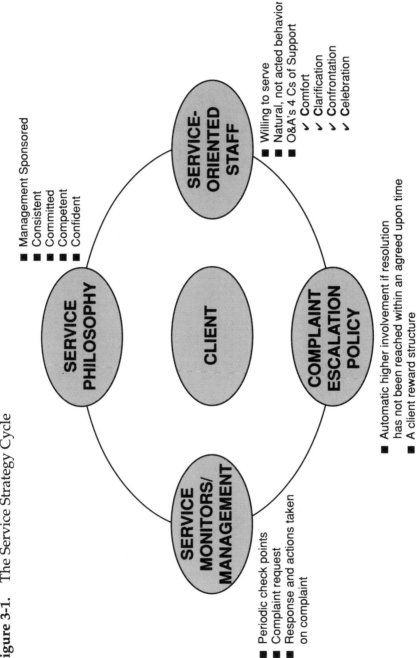

The philosophy needs to emphasize the 4 Cs:

- Consistent
- Committed
- Competent
- Confident

If any of the four Cs are missing, it will show. Your clients will know and your service level will probably be lower than desired.

Let's look back at each of the Cs now to show their importance and explain how they relate to I.S.

Consistency can be a danger if emphasized in an insincere manner.

Consistency

Look at the major fast-food chains—McDonald's, Burger King, and Wendy's. In each one, you know what you'll get for service, whether it's in Taos, New Mexico or Lewiston, Maine. You can predict your interaction with the salesperson. You can even predict the layout of the building. Now I'm not commenting on the quality of their service, only on their consistency.

Consistency can be a danger if emphasized in an insincere manner. A year ago I checked into a first-class hotel and was greeted by a bellman who said, "Happy to serve you, sir." After checking me in, the woman at the reception desk said, "Happy to serve you, sir." Another bellman took my bags to my room and after receiving his tip said, "Happy to serve you, sir." I went to the restaurant for a snack. When returning my credit card, the waitress said, "Happy to serve you, sir." The next morning my wake-up call came. I said "thank you," then, before the receptionist had a chance to speak, I said, "I know, you're happy to serve me." These people had been trained, but it wasn't coming naturally, it wasn't sincere. In I.S. as well, we want consistency but we don't want robots. We need belief in the values of service. If we're consistent with our clients, then they will know how to read us. They know what to expect. And in I.S. we're not yet known for that consistency.

Committed

Being really committed is seeing professionals who are committed to their jobs and show it. Behaving like savvy internal consultant, when they are confronted by angry clients, they don't take the wrath personally, don't become defensive or make excuses—they simply listen, and then ask to hear more. They are committed to hang in there for a successful outcome.

Competent

Staffers who deal most often with clients must be competent to carry out their jobs. They are skilled, experienced professionals conscious that they are conveying an image for the entire IS organization. Competent enough to advise the client of another alternative if need be.

Confident

Internal I.S. consultants should never be arrogant, but clearly demonstrate confidence in their expertise and their ability to solve problems and provide excellent service.

Be Willing to Serve

The next position in our Service Cycle is a crucial one. It deals with our Service-Oriented Staff. To succeed, they must be willing to serve. Service should come naturally. Think of the supermarket checkout person who slurs the "Thank you for shopping with us. Have a good day." The words lose their meaning. Instead of convincing you to return, the way the words are said makes you think that the employees aren't trained appropriately, or aren't motivated. It creates an indifference in your attitude toward the store, and we saw earlier how indifference is a primary reason why people don't return to buy or use your service again.

Look beyond the words. Did you create a picture of that checkout person in your mind? Describe the posture, the expression on the face. The impression someone else has of you goes far beyond the words. In fact, studies have shown that only 3% to 7% of communication between people is in the words themselves. Your attitude shows in everything you do.

Along with the 4 Cs of Service Philosophy discussed earlier, we now present you with the 4 Cs of support.

- Comfort
- Clarification
- Confrontation
- Celebration

All four of these Cs apply to both you and your client. However, you need to set an atmosphere conducive to the 4 Cs. You and your client must both be **comfortable** as you analyze the problem and devise a solution. Everything must be clear. If either side doesn't understand a point, **clarify.** Also, discussion should be in language appropriate to the other person. If the client won't understand your jargon, don't use it. It doesn't show off your intelligence; it confuses your client. These guidelines apply whether you're working together to plan a solution to a problem or handling a complaint.

Confrontation is meeting the issue head-on. Don't skirt the key point. Don't tackle the easy part and put off the difficult. And when you're through, when the problem is solved or the issue resolved, thank the other person, congratulate the other people on the team for a job well done. If it's the end of a major job that's taken weeks or months to complete, perhaps a more formal **celebration** is in order, from gathering people together at the end of the day for pizza or simply saying, "Let's celebrate a job well done."

Return to Complaint Management

Continuing clockwise, Complaint Escalation Policy is next. This is a very important part of the service strategy. It defines what process will occur when a customer complains. If a problem is not resolved within a specified time, then higher involvement (not excluding prayer) should be automatic. You set the parameters that are best for your situation. For example, if a problem can't be handled in half an hour, perhaps it then goes to the next level of expertise or of management.

If there's no escalation policy in effect, here's what frequently happens. Imagine yourself in a different company department or in a store making what you consider to be a simple complaint. You state your case, to be met by someone who merely repeats, "that's the way we do things," or "it's policy," ad nauseam. To break the repetitive chain, you finally ask to speak to the manager. Regardless of the resolution, you're left with an unpleasant taste in your mouth. It would have been so much better for the person to have understood your point of view, and upon realizing that he was unable to help, to call in another person without you having to request it.

A client reward structure should also be in place. You want the client not only to feel that the problem is solved, but also to feel positive about the way it was handled. She's more likely to return than if there hadn't been a problem at all. Professional understanding (without any condescension) sets the tone. Involvement of the manager, when appropriate, shows the importance of the client and her problem.

If the problem was either caused by I.S. or equally by I.S. and the client, why not give the client something to make up for the time and trouble she's gone through. Perhaps a couple free hours of consulting or training? Definitely not a key chain with the company logo. If the problem was the result of client carelessness or error, don't reward her. But also, don't berate her; she probably feels badly enough already about wasting your time and hers. Even in this situation, the client should always be treated with respect, as the valued client that she is.

Managing the Process

The final stop around the Service Strategy Cycle is Service Monitors & Service Management. It's not enough to put the plan into action. You must assure that it's running smoothly. Be sure that service records are being kept, not only of projects, but of questions and complaints that come in. Schedule periodic check points where

- Records will be reviewed
- Complaints will be evaluated
- Specific actions will be reconsidered
- Staff will discuss how the system is working, and
- Staff will see if we're meeting the goals we set for level of service.

Models of Service

What model of service do you try to provide? Is it the same as you actually give? There are basically three levels of service for us to consider: economy, satisfaction, and care. These models are designed for reflection as to which model you may be utilizing. To ask, "Is this the right model for us to use?" There are no 100% answers that say one model is the one you should use, but some of the models clearly lend themselves more towards a client service-orientation. The chart in Figure 3-2 is a handy reference to the levels.

The Economy Model

Many I.S. programs operate on the economy model. People in them are likely to say that it's not by choice. They're forced into the economy plan by management or the corporate financial picture. "We're understaffed. We wish we could expand our service but, . . . maybe in the future." Or "We're lean and mean. That's the way to run an organization. No fat. In these tough economic times it's the only way to be. When the economy picks up, then we'll look at adding services, but not now."

Their focus is on transactions, on the here and now. How many transactions can we process in a day? Let's do the job quickly and right so we can move on. Note that they do want to do things right. And the focus on speed appears to match the current business buzz phrase, "Time-Based Management," coined by George Stalk in the mid 80's. Most time-based management proponents will say now that competitors have quality, quality is no longer a competitive advantage. Therefore, the new goal is to retain the highest level of quality, while doing it faster. The difference between Time-Based Management and the economy level of service is that economy doesn't go for "the highest level of quality." It looks to reduce time, reduce effort, reduce personal involvement—reduction everywhere.

In the economy level, the client is viewed as a consumer. He's just the person or group that utilizes your work—there's nothing personal, no relationship to build.

The Satisfaction Model

In the satisfaction model, there's more focus on the customer. That's a slightly warmer word—customer. It implies an individuality, unlike the amorphous consumer. You work to make everything convenient for the customer.

The goal is to meet specifications. At the economy level, you'll also try to meet specifications, but the targeted speed and efficiency is likely to mean that those specs will slip occasionally. The customer deserves Quality with a capital "Q." "We aim to deliver everything the customer wants."

That all sounds pretty good. If you were the customer in such a situation, you'd be pleased, wouldn't you, because it's better than what you're accustomed to? An everyday example of the satisfaction level is the convenience store. There are several successful chains, and their names, often with "convenient" or "convenience" in them, indicate their main quality. You know you'll pay a little more, and you know the selection won't be as wide, but they're convenient. They know how to meet specifications. The customer quickly needs milk and diapers. They're handy, as is the store—specs met. And the quality of the product is good.

Here's a situation to analyze for level of service. You're interested in upgrading several of your printers. You visit the vendors so you can see several models. Each is set up for convenient access in a reasonably attractive area. The courteous, attentive salesperson listens to your needs, directly addresses them, and recommends model XJ2-731P. You agree, and everyone is pleased. What could be better?

The Care Model

Here's what's better, someone who cares. Take a moment to think how that printer salesperson could have been even better. It's so easy to be happy with what's a bit above the norm, but how could he have exceeded your expectations? Think of specific things he could have done better. Write down your ideas. Then come back and match them up with the ones I'll give. You'll probably have a few that I haven't listed and that's great!

Here's my list of how the salesperson could have exceeded your expectations.

1. Do research. If the salesperson knows you're coming in and his company has worked with you before, there should be past records. He should know what equipment you currently have, who your previous salesperson was, when you previously purchased, and what service or maintenance has been provided.

2. Go beyond needs that you, the customer, are aware of. The salesperson's first obligation is to listen. You can state those uses that you know of, but the salesperson should have knowledge of how others are using each model, and access to information about coming technology. "Have you thought of the advantages of a color printer?" "Do you need to connect to your oblong widget?" "Might you want this printer to serve a network in the future?" Try to anticipate the possible needs.

3. Ask about how and where it's used. What's the level of use? The cleanliness of the area? These may make a difference in recommending the right model.

4. Ask if someone will be needed to set it up?

5. Ask about training needs. If there are advanced features, the salesperson should warn you about how the majority of users only use a small fraction of the features, and that training can significantly improve efficiency.

6. Find out if there is a need for paper, extra ribbons, or anything else?

7. Ask what your plan is for maintenance. The salesperson should advise about the recommended maintenance.

8. Follow up. He should call you in a week to see if installation went smoothly and the equipment is operating properly.

It's interesting to note that being more pro-active and responsive to your client is also setting the stage for a strong, long-term relationship.

The goal here is to build a relationship that's based on mutual respect and trust. The buyer will return because the salesperson cares about him as an individual, and works "above and beyond" to help. The buyer is no longer a consumer or a customer but is now a client, someone with whom the salesperson is building an ongoing relationship. "Added Value" is provided. Not only are the stated concerns addressed, but other concerns are anticipated. The success of the Care Level of service extends beyond just "doing" all these extras. The attitude must be genuine and sincere. No slick salespeople need apply.

Now go back to the question, "What level of service do you provide?" Very few I.S. departments are consistently at the Care Level. The question then becomes, how do we analyze ourselves, and how do we improve? Read on.

Figure 3-2.

SERVICE LEVEL CHOICES

	ECONOMY	SATISFACTION	CARE
FOCUS	Transactions	Convenience	Relationship
GOAL	Speed and Efficiency	Meet Specifications	Exceed Expectations
STRATEGY	Reduction	Quality	Added Value
VIEWPOINT	Consumer	Customer	Client

PERSONAL ACTION PLAN

Worksheet

THE SERVICE STRATEGY CYCLE

Specific ideas I can use on the job:

Specific actions I will take within 30 days:

Chapter 4

Assess Your Service Level

"Negative expectation thwarts realization, and self-congratulation guarantees disaster."

—*Michael Donner*

How to Use the Assessment Tools

We have designed two service level assessment tools to help you evaluate your current service position. One is for you to complete; the other is designed to be completed by your clients. You're welcome to duplicate these tools. They're on separate pages to make it easier for you to use them. If you adapt my format or any of my questions into your own assessment tool, all I ask is that you give printed and verbal credit to Ouellette & Associates.

Self-Assessment

This first tool is for self-assessment. Even if you're reading this book alone, I recommend that you make two copies of this tool, which is in Figure 4-1. Use one copy to assess yourself. Use the other to assess how you see your entire department of the I.S. organization.

If you use separate sheets, then you can continue to refer to them as you read the rest of the book and devise your own strategies for improvement.

Using the Self Assessment Tool put your name at the top, and circle the number that indicates your impression of your client service effectiveness. There are 25 questions. When you finish, first record your scores on the Self-Assessment Tally form, Figure 4-2. If your answer to #1 is 3, put a 3 after "1" under the heading "Responsiveness." If you answered a 2 on #2, then a 2 goes next to "2" under "Assurance." After transferring all the scores, add each column.

Then transfer your totals from each column to the Self-Assessment Summary, Figure 4-3. If your total under "Responsiveness" on the Self-Assessment Tally is 14, then place a dot on the Summary at 14 under the "Responsiveness" heading. Connect the dots and you'll have a visual interpretation of your score.

Figure 4-1. Self Assessment Tool—I.S. Client Service Level

Name

Circle the number that matches your impression of your organization's client service effectiveness.

	Never	Seldom	Sometimes	Often	Always
1. We are responsive to our clients.	0	1	2	3	4
2. We listen carefully and ask clarifying questions to help understand what others are saying.	0	1	2	3	4
3. We deliver projects that have few problems.	0	1	2	3	4
4. We do it right the first time.	0	1	2	3	4
5. We spend time with our clients to fully understand their business needs.	0	1	2	3	4

Figure 4-1. Self Assessment Tool—I.S. Client Service Level
(*continued*)

	Never	Seldom	Sometimes	Often	Always
6. We respond promptly to client questions and needs.	0	1	2	3	4
7. We explain technical issues thoroughly, in a way which helps clients understand more easily.	0	1	2	3	4
8. We are usually on target in addressing client business needs with effective technology/ approaches.	0	1	2	3	4
9. We deliver what we have committed to.	0	1	2	3	4
10. We work hard to provide clients with individual attention.	0	1	2	3	4
11. We respond effectively to difficult situations rather than avoiding them.	0	1	2	3	4
12. We explain things to clients so that they may learn from us.	0	1	2	3	4
13. We consider alternatives and look for value-added solutions.	0	1	2	3	4
14. We understand our clients' business needs.	0	1	2	3	4
15. We know when and how to say no.	0	1	2	3	4
16. We are willing to help our clients in whatever way we can.	0	1	2	3	4
17. We ask good questions of our clients and thoroughly explain why we need the answers.	0	1	2	3	4
18. We deliver products that are efficient and effective.	0	1	2	3	4
19. We get work done in a timely manner.	0	1	2	3	4

Figure 4-1.   Self Assessment Tool—I.S. Client Service Level
(continued)

	Never	Seldom	Sometimes	Often	Always
20. We go out of our way to make sure clients are satisfied.	0	1	2	3	4
21. We follow up with clients on inquiries, problems, and always gauge their satisfaction.	0	1	2	3	4
22. We take considerable time to assess needs, the situation and the problems before responding with a recommendation.	0	1	2	3	4
23. We make recommendations our clients trust.	0	1	2	3	4
24. We stand behind our products and services.	0	1	2	3	4
25. We take advantage of opportunities to learn about our clients and their business.	0	1	2	3	4

Figure 4-2. Self-Assessment Tally

Name _____

Insert scores for questions 1–25 below and total each column.

Self-Assessment Tally

RESPONSIVENESS	ASSURANCE	TANGIBLES	RELIABILITY	EMPATHY
1. _3_	2. ____	3. ____	4. ____	5. ____
6. _4_	7. ____	8. ____	9. ____	10. ____
11. _2_	12. ____	13. ____	14. ____	15. ____
16. _3_	17. ____	18. ____	19. ____	20. ____
21. _2_	22. ____	23. ____	24. ____	25. ____
Totals: _14_	____	____	____	____

Figure 4-3. Self-Assessment Summary

Chart the above totals below for a visual graph of SERVICE strengths/weaknesses:

Responsiveness	Assurance	Tangibles	Reliability	Empathy
20	20	20	20	20
—	—	—	—	—
—	—	—	—	—
15	15	15	15	15
—	—	—	—	—
—	—	—	—	—
10	10	10	10	10
—	—	—	—	—
—	—	—	—	—
5	5	5	5	5
—	—	—	—	—
—	—	—	—	—
0	0	0	0	0

Self-Assessment Grid

Interpreting the Self-Assessments

Ideally, your entire department will participate in this Self-Assessment. You can benefit from tabulations of both the individual self-assessment (what each person thinks of his own work), and the group self-assessment (how each person sees the entire department). No one should be required to discuss or admit to his self-assessment, but it's revealing to see if, as a group, the individuals view themselves as better than or poorer than the group as a whole.

It's useful to compare your responses against some typical results. Based on the many service level assessments I've conducted, here are the items that people standardly score themselves the lowest on.

5. Spend time with my clients to fully understand their business needs.
7. Explain technical issues thoroughly, in a way which helps clients understand more easily.
21. Follow up with clients on inquiries, problems, and always gauge their satisfaction.
22. Take considerable time to assess needs, the situation and the problems before responding with a recommendation.
25. Take advantage of opportunities to learn about my clients and their business.

In all of these typical shortfall areas, time is involved. Most I.S. people prefer to be working on technical problems rather than working with clients. Most IPPs have excellent technical backgrounds, so that's naturally what they want to stress over their management backgrounds or people skills. This reinforces the basis for the I.S. stereotype. It'll take a good deal of effort to change that perception.

All these questions that usually have the weakest answers require a person who genuinely likes being with people, and who enjoys understanding all aspects of the problems he faces: that's technical, business, and human problems. Our education process, the computer science curriculum at major universities, is starting to include the business and human sides more strongly, but for those of us on the job, we've got to learn them and apply them now.

I.S. needs to find measurable ways to evaluate its success.

Before and After

The time involved in these typically low-scoring areas falls into two slots—before and after the "real development work" occurs. #21 is one of the hardest to do, and not because it's so difficult.

21. Follow up with clients on inquiries, problems, and always gauge their satisfaction.

Once a project is "over," it's hard to make time to do follow-up work. There are new problems to be solved. That problem is done with. Yet how do you truly know how well you've done unless you've checked back in periodically to see how your application or solution is doing?

Think of your own education. You would study, you would cram, and you would get a respectable grade. But then what would happen if what you had memorized wasn't used in the near future. Usually, you'd forget the details, maybe remembering a couple basic principles. The same procedure applies here.

For example, in a training situation in your company, the trainer is only successful if the new learning is applied on the job. That means carefully selecting the time for the training, just before the content material is needed, and following up afterwards to learn how well it is being applied. And there should be a means of measuring how much the training has influenced behavior change.

In the same way, I.S. needs to find measurable ways to evaluate its success. Show that productivity is improved. Work with the client to develop the means of measurement, because the client will also benefit from positive results.

Key Points:

Items #5, #22 and #25 all involve preliminary work. Americans are so action-oriented that when we see a problem we usually want to jump right in. Let's re-read these three items:

> 5. Spend time with my clients to fully understand their business needs.
> 22. Take considerable time to assess needs, the situation and the problems before responding with a recommendation.
> 25. Take advantage of opportunities to learn about my clients and their business.

Each of these involves the Caring Level of service. Doing these will help build a relationship with your client. Take the time to learn more of the business behind the task you're working on. If you do, you'll almost certainly exceed expectations, and you'll be adding value because of the increased depth of your knowledge.

Take the time to do the appropriate preliminary analysis of your problem, and take the time to follow-up on the longer range results of your work. You'll learn more about the entire business, and develop stronger relationships with other groups. That's service.

Evaluation Categories

Our Self-Assessment Tally and Summary divide your answers into five categories:*

- ■ Responsiveness
- ■ Assurance
- ■ Tangibles
- ■ Reliability
- ■ Empathy

*We took our five categories from the Texas A&M University study, "What Clients Really Want," and then developed our assessment tools.

If any one or two areas stand out as being especially strong, congratulations. If any one or two are especially weak, it's time to concentrate on them. But before taking any action, compare your results with those on the Client Feedback Assessment Tool of I.S. Service. We will come back to the five categories in Chapter 5.

Client Feedback Assessment

The Self-Assessment demonstrated what you think of your own service level. The Client Feedback Assessment Tool, Figure 4-4, is designed to show what your client thinks of it. As before, you're welcome to duplicate this tool. Following The Client Feedback Assessment Tool, there's a Tally and a Summary to show results.

This tool may also be used in two ways. One is for you to put on the hat of typical clients and answer as you think they would answer. These results can then be compared with your own Self-Assessment. This will show where *you* believe that you and clients see things alike and differently.

Then distribute the tool to a number of clients representing differing kinds of work for the I.S. organization. Three representative clients should indicate the variation and consistency in client responses. The clients should be from different departments and different locations with which you work. And don't give the assessment tool only to those you know were pleased with the I.S. department's work. You may be tempted to avoid someone who wasn't pleased, because there were "extraneous circumstances" and you don't want the survey skewed. On the contrary, you want a fully representative sampling.

Figure 4-4. Client Feedback Assessment Tool—I.S. Service Level

---

Name

Circle the number that matches your impression of the service you
receive from I.S.

	Never	Seldom	Sometimes	Often	Always
1. I.S. is responsive to me as a client.	0	1	2	3	4
2. I.S. listens carefully and asks clarifying questions to help understand what they are saying.	0	1	2	3	4
3. I.S. delivers projects that have few problems.	0	1	2	3	4
4. I.S. does it right the first time.	0	1	2	3	4
5. I.S. spends time with me to fully understand my business needs.	0	1	2	3	4
6. I.S. responds promptly to my questions and needs.	0	1	2	3	4
7. I.S. explains technical issues thoroughly and in a way which helps me understand more easily.	0	1	2	3	4
8. I.S. is usually on target in addressing my business needs with effective technology.	0	1	2	3	4
9. I.S. delivers what they have committed to.	0	1	2	3	4
10. I.S. works hard to provide individual attention.	0	1	2	3	4
11. I.S. responds effectively to difficult situations rather than avoiding them.	0	1	2	3	4
12. I.S. explains things in such a way that I learn from them.	0	1	2	3	4
13. I.S. considers alternatives and looks for value-added solutions.	0	1	2	3	4

Figure 4-4. Client Feedback Assessment Tool—I.S. Service Level (*continued*)

	Never	Seldom	Sometimes	Often	Always
14. I.S. understands my business needs.	0	1	2	3	4
15. I.S. knows when and how to say no.	0	1	2	3	4
16. I.S. demonstrates a willingness to help.	0	1	2	3	4
17. I.S. asks good questions and thoroughly explains why they need the answers.	0	1	2	3	4
18. I.S. delivers products that are efficient and effective.	0	1	2	3	4
19. I.S. gets work done in a timely manner.	0	1	2	3	4
20. I.S. goes out of their way to make sure I am satisfied.	0	1	2	3	4
21. I.S. follows up with me on inquiries, problems, and always gauges my satisfaction.	0	1	2	3	4
22. I.S. takes considerable time assessing my needs and situation and problems, before responding with a recommendation.	0	1	2	3	4
23. I.S. makes recommendations I can trust.	0	1	2	3	4
24. I.S. stands behind their products and services.	0	1	2	3	4
25. I.S. takes advantage of opportunities to learn about me and my business.	0	1	2	3	4

Figure 4-5. Client Feedback Assessment Tally—I.S. Service Level

Name

Insert the score received on questions 1–25, from each of the three respondents in the spaces provided below. (Allows survey responses for up to three clients)

Client Assessment Tally

RESPONSIVENESS	ASSURANCE	TANGIBLES	RELIABILITY	EMPATHY
1. __ __ __	2. __ __ __	3. __ __ __	4. __ __ __	5. __ __ __
6. __ __ __	7. __ __ __	8. __ __ __	9. __ __ __	10. __ __ __
11. __ __ __	12. __ __ __	13. __ __ __	14. __ __ __	15. __ __ __
16. __ __ __	17. __ __ __	18. __ __ __	19. __ __ __	20. __ __ __
21. __ __ __	22. __ __ __	23. __ __ __	24. __ __ __	25. __ __ __
Totals: __ __	__ __	__	__	__
Avges: __	__	__	__	__

Figure 4-6. Client Assessment Summary

Chart tally averages below* for a visual graph of SERVICE strengths/weaknesses:

Responsiveness	Assurance	Tangibles	Reliability	Empathy
20 ||||	20 ||||	20 ||||	20 ||||	20 ||||
15 ||||	15 ||||	15 ||||	15 ||||	15 ||||
10 ||||	10 ||||	10 ||||	10 ||||	10 ||||
5 ||||	5 ||||	5 ||||	5 ||||	5 ||||
0	0	0	0	0

Client Assessment Grid

*Client responses 1, 2, 3.

Notice that the Client Assessment Summary has three places to record answers. So if you surveyed three clients, all their responses will be visible on one Tally form.

After the clients' responses to the Client Assessment Summary are tabulated, there are several ways to review the results. Check how consistent the responses are from your clients. This will indicate such things as whether

- All clients are being treated alike
- All IPPs are following the same procedures
- All the problems are equally well understood.

Then compare the Client Assessment Summary results with the Self-Assessment results. Are you in sync with your clients? When the tools show that your perceptions are quite different, you must determine the reasons for the differing perceptions. Whenever the reasons for client comments are not clear, you should arrange to meet with clients to understand their concerns. This may be done in meetings with individuals, or it may be in focus groups of five or six clients.

What's Holding Us Back?

One other analysis that's necessary is to look at each question and say, "What's preventing us from being a "4"? Some of you will say, "Here we go again. Motherhood, apple pie, and a perfect world. Can't happen." I say again that you can seriously believe that a 4 is attainable, and that you won't ever get there unless you expect to get there.

To help you see where problems can arise, I have yet another form called, "Rating the Potential Daily Business Negatives to Good Client Service." The rating system remains the same, 0 to 4 ranging from "Never" to "Always." How often do each of the potential problems listed keep you from performing at a "4" level? This time, though, your goal is a "0" in each category.

Figure 4-7. Rating the Potential Daily Business Negatives to Good Client Service

	Never	Seldom	Sometimes	Often	Always
	0	1	2	3	4
Conflicting agendas					
Preconceived solution (client)					
Preconceived solution (us)					
Budget					
Resources					
Personalities					
Perceptions					
Department commitment					
Clarity of roles					
Mid-course corrections					
Consistent standards (procedures, methodologies)					
Information delivered or heard incorrectly					
Vendors					
Follow-through (client)					
Follow-through (us)					
Physical setup					
Training					
Other problems (be precise)					

Take a close look at the results here. This should provide you with some of the key elements that are preventing you from providing excellent client service. Extract those negatives from the list and start formulating plans to eliminate them or at least put strategies in place to minimize them.

Once you have responded to those potential problems, some of which certainly overlap, go back and select the two that are the greatest problems. Then go back and select the number one problem. This is what you especially need to work on.

Force Field Analysis

A force field analysis can help you as you plan solutions to your greatest problem, selected from the list above. Here's how it works.

Put one of your major problem areas on the top, so that it's listed as a negative force, pushing you down. Beneath the horizontal line, start listing what needs to be done to resolve the problem. These are forces pushing up. You need to make the positive forces the stronger. You need to enact them. This doesn't show you how to enact them, but it's a simple representation of your problem and your potential solutions.

Figure 4-8.

Force Field Analysis
− 1
− 2   List negative forces
− 3
.
.
────────────────────────────
+ 1
+ 2
+ 3   List positive forces, (not benefits)
.
.
.

Sharing Results

When all of your analysis is done and you've determined any needed plan of action, be sure to share your plans with those who filled out the Client Feedback Assessment. If you don't, they're likely to think that their survey vanished into a great wasteland. Sharing the information is both good public relations and helps to build a credible relationship with our clients.

Applying Your Assessments

You've spent this chapter assessing your service level. To apply the results effectively, you need to understand what your clients want. That's the topic of the next chapter. To prepare for it, make your own list now of what you believe your clients really want. What makes clients know that they're getting good service? We'll use it in Chapter 5.

PERSONAL ACTION PLAN

Worksheet

ASSESS YOUR SERVICE LEVEL

Specific ideas I can use on the job:

Specific actions I will take within 30 days:

Chapter 5

What Clients Really Want

"Asking the right questions takes as much skill as giving the right answers."

—*Robert Half*

Understanding Your Clients' Needs

You ended Chapter 4 by writing down what you believe your clients most value in your service. Many of you probably wrote down qualities much like the categories of answers on the Service Assessment Tools you'd just been working with. They are the five categories that, in general, clients want most.

- Responsiveness
- Assurance
- Tangibles
- Reliability
- Empathy

Are any of these five not on your own list? You can certainly have other names for the same concepts. For example, "Tangibles" includes "Neat Appearance" and "Clean Work Area." If you're totally missing a category, it's time for a little soul-searching. Why didn't you see that as important to your client? Let's expand on these terms and how they relate to us.

Responsiveness

Here's a listing of behaviors you should have if you're appropriately responsive to your clients.* This may start out resembling the Boy Scout Oath, which is not a bad model to have in mind.

- Be helpful
- Be prompt
- Don't keep clients waiting
- Be accessible and available
- Be willing to help clients whenever they have problems
- Keep clients informed
- Provide the service as soon as possible
- Anticipate

These qualities of Responsiveness seem simple when printed out. They're so basic, so logical. But how often have we avoided calling back a client? How often have we had information that our client could have profitably used, but we neglected to pass it on in a timely manner? I understand that we have a number of clients to serve, and there's a lot of prioritizing to be done. We can't be accessible to everyone all the time. But providing service "as soon as possible" may not be for an extended period. What should we do? Remember that it is not saying "no" or delaying the client that is the major problem but rather how we handle this sensitive transaction.

The final item on the Responsiveness list, "anticipate," calls out for special attention. We all know how difficult it is for some clients to verbalize their needs. This is especially true at the upper levels of management with senior executives who aren't familiar with computers, or perhaps how computers can best be used in their workaday world. We should have sufficient familiarity with their needs so that we can bring them ideas on how to improve their work.

---

*We've adapted and expanded the listing of traits in each of the five categories from the Texas A&M study.

Studies have estimated that only 2% of senior corporate executives use computer technology on a regular basis in the performance of their duties. This excludes computer uses like E mail and maintaining a calendar. Contrary to our belief that executives prefer to delegate computer usage or that they are too busy to learn the technology, the executives claim that they clearly see the value of computerization for them but that we (I.S.) have been ineffective at bringing into the corporate environment the related type of information they need to formulate good business decisions. We have not effectively focused on the value-added benefits we can produce.

Assurance

Is your behavior toward your client such that the client has full confidence in you? Here are actions that promote that desired level of assurance:

- Be knowledgeable
- Be courteous
- Project confidence
- Provide peace of mind
- Be trustworthy
- Be a sincere helper
- Be an advocate of your client
- Have no hidden costs
- Deliver security with integrity
- Lower the risks and dangers
- Provide guarantees

That last one—provide guarantees—scares a lot of people. Many hesitate to offer guarantees because they know that for some projects the results may be beyond their control. But think what providing guarantees may do. It may well force us to look at all aspects of a project more clearly, including likely delays, interruptions, and cost overruns. We'd be forced to add contingency time to the project. We would probably try to be more realistic, and to discuss that realistic outlook with the client. And that realism on our part means the client would tend to have realistic expectations that we can live up to.

I know the fears of this approach, but if we are to build credibility and compete (yes, compete), we need to address this issue. Examples of possible guarantees are: absorbing the overrun cost, providing additional enhancements free, and providing additional systems analysis or support services. Get creative. You'll be surprised how much a creative guarantee policy will enhance client service.

Assurance also helps to put clients at ease. They should feel confident that they're in good hands, that you'll be looking out for their interests. That's key. Interdivisional rivalries are keen in many organizations. Because we deal with so many departments, we can be an important factor in bringing everyone together, in promoting a sense of teamwork, a sense of "We're all in this together, so let's work with mutual respect for each other's skills to make the entire system better."

Are you genuinely looking out for clients' interests now? Consistently? Think again of those areas most IPPs score lowest on in the self-assessment. You must take the time to understand your client's problem.

How can you lower the risks and dangers? Be open with clients. Let them know their options related to both finance and performance. Recommend the best route for them, and clearly explain why. And what will happen if something doesn't turn out as expected? Let them know what you'll do to rectify the situation and what it's likely to cost. Nothing hidden. No surprises. We know our work well and must project that comfortable confidence in a relaxed yet efficient manner.

Tangibles

Take a look around your department. Imagine that you're a new manufacturing manager with a problem, and you're arriving for a meeting to discuss it. This is your first visit to I.S. What do you see? Are there papers stuck everywhere on the walls? Are books and magazines piled up on the floor? Is the telephone buried on your desk? Do you feel welcome? Does the department reflect the right image? Can anything be improved? Tangibles create the first impression, and that first impression is hard to dislodge. Are all these tangibles as you want them?

- Attractive facilities
- Clean and functional equipment
- People who are well-groomed
- First class-image

If those first four traits are not readily evident, how difficult will it be to make changes? Properly approached, your staff will most likely agree with these service "tangibles."

"Well-groomed" needs comment. In most companies, the days of the dress code are gone. Just realize that you can be casual without being sloppy. Our clients will partially judge us on how we appear, whether that's indicative of our work habits or not.

We often consider our area as a "shop." There's nothing wrong with that image. It's a homey sound, small and comfortable. But it may not be appropriate to be in a shop, when all around us are in departments. Perhaps a shop indicates a group of tinkerers, rather than professionals. Perhaps thinking of ourselves as a shop creates an unnecessary division between us and the rest of the organization. The mind set is what's important here, not the name we use, but sometimes the name reflects the mind set.

Reliability

We've seen that "Responsiveness" describes how quickly and effectively you react to client needs. "Assurance" has to do with the image, attitude and skills you have and project. "Tangibles" need to reflect that assurance. "Reliability" has to do with our performance.

Some I.S. departments in the past based everything on performance. As long as the job was done right, who cared if you were nice? You were the guru who had "the answer," and "they" bowed before the altar of your knowledge. In the new environment, working as a team with our clients, there's a danger of focusing so heavily on cooperation that attention to performance gets sacrificed. This danger is partly from overcompensating for the excesses of the past, and partly from being distracted by the newer human aspects of technology so you feel there's no time for real technical work any more.

Your ultimate reputation still depends on how your deliverables work. IPPs must be just as analytically and technically sound as they've always been. They just need a myriad of additional "people skills," too. Juggling it all together may take some time to learn.

To be considered reliable, we need to:

- Be dependable
- Be accurate
- Be consistent
- Not make promises we can't keep
- Do what we say we are going to do
- Do it when we say we are going to do it
- Get it done on time
- DIRTFT (Do It Right The First Time)

Always be honest. Don't necessarily tell people what they expect to hear. Tell them the truth. Do the necessary upfront research so that you'll not only Do It Right, but you'll Do It Right The First Time, and that first time will be on time.

Empathy

The last of the five categories is Empathy. The first two categories, Responsiveness and Assurance, are also people skills, however, they're both easier to accomplish than Empathy. Responsiveness and Assurance are more process-driven; they're easier to learn. Empathy is much harder to learn. It comes from within, and is defined as:

- Providing individual attention
- Listening actively
- Treating the client as someone special
- Putting on the client's glasses (hat, shoes)
- Feeling what the client is feeling
- Asking questions
- Using the client's language
- Customizing
- Treating the client the way the client wants to be treated

The traits for "Responsiveness" begin like the Boy Scout Oath. Looking back on "Assurance," many of those traits are those also needed by the local pastor or family doctor. "Empathy" appears to be a blend of Mr. Rogers and "The Golden Rule". But no one is trying to mold IPPs into superhuman beings. The lists only look overpowering when they're viewed as lists. When they're viewed as behaviors they fold together into a way of working that, in general, comes naturally to most people.

Listening has been mentioned before. Your client is the star. Without the client, we have no business. Really *Listen* to what the client says. That's easier said than done.

Testing for Empathy

Let's look at an example. One of your clients comes to you and says that she went out and bought a PC-based relational database system to solve one of their problems. They've input all their data and it does fill the need. But now they need to work that newly developed data into information on the corporate database, and the client can't see any way to do it and so comes to you. What's your reaction?

I.S. Delivers Reliable C.A.R.E.

Quite likely you tell the client that she made a mistake. While the software she bought solves her specific problem, it simply can't connect to the corporate database. If she'd come to you at first, you could have designed a software solution that would have the needed connectivity, but now she'll have to have all the needed new data re-keyed if it's going into the corporate database.

How good is that response? Is it accurate? honest? fair? Take a look at the listing above for empathy. Are all those directives being followed? Did you listen to the subtext, the words behind the words? How about "Put on the client glasses" and "Feel what the client is feeling?"

You began by saying the wrong thing to your client. She didn't "make a mistake." Don't begin by telling her she's wrong and you're right. She probably felt, based on past experience or rumors, that I.S. couldn't address their needs, either in terms of a simple solution or time. The ComputerLand or BusinessLand salesperson in the store around the corner did her job by telling your client that all she has to do is buy this software and the problem will be solved.

And this example doesn't even go as far as such a case often does. If the software bombs, the client will come to you and say, "I need help. This software isn't behaving as it's supposed to. Please support it." How are you going to support a package when you don't even know what it does? You can't be expected to know about everything.

In this database example, there's no easy answer. But with appropriate empathy, understanding of the situation, you'll leave your client feeling that she isn't dumb, or wrong, or alienating you, and you won't alienate her. And she may well believe that you're her best source for service in the future.

Words to Live By

I. S. DELIVERS RELIABLE C.A.R.E.

The last two words in this sentence capture all five categories from the Service Self-Assessment and Client Feedback surveys. Let me explain. CARE is an acronym standing for the following:

"C" is "Confidence," the same as "Assurance"
"A" is "Appeal," what's created by proper use of "Tangibles"
"R" is "Responsiveness"
"E" is "Empathy"

I'm not suggesting that you necessarily take this as a slogan and post it around the building, but you should be practicing it. If you do deliver Reliable C.A.R.E., you know it, and your clients will, too.

PERSONAL ACTION PLAN

Worksheet

WHAT CLIENTS REALLY WANT

Specific ideas I can use on the job:

Specific actions I will take within 30 days:

Chapter 6

Myths and Sins

"An important task of a manager is to reduce his people's excuses for failure."

—*Robert Townsend*

Excuses, Excuses

This chapter will take a look at excuses, so if you never make any you can skip directly to Chapter 7. A couple excuses were offered back on page 37 when I discussed the economy level of service. Such excuses can more kindly be called rationalizations. But who wants to be kind? My goal is to wipe out the excuses that inhibit good service.

12 Client Service Myths

We have identified twelve typical myths that seem to prevent us from providing the right atmosphere for good client service. Timid IPPs consistently use them to hide behind. Let's dispel each myth once and for all.

> **My goal is to wipe out the excuses that inhibit good service.**

Myth #1. Clients Don't Know What They Want.

This parallels a complaint about clients in just about every arena. If we're the experts, then it's probably true. *In terms of our knowledge,* clients don't know what they want. But then, if they had our knowledge, they wouldn't need our help.

This situation is why outstanding service is not defined as "giving the client exactly what he wants." The client probably does not know all the options, doesn't know how the widget can be used in other ways, doesn't know what the next generation of product will bring, doesn't know what he can hook his widget up to.

Often there's a language problem, as well as a knowledge problem. You might say, "Clients can't describe their own needs in terminology that I can understand." A client might say of you, "He always speaks in technical terms that I don't fully understand, but I feel that I'm stupid if I ask, so I keep quiet." It's the proverbial two-way street. The client shouldn't toss around business terms that we don't know, and we shouldn't use technical jargon.

Often the client doesn't know what he doesn't know. He may come to us with a precise laundry list and say, "I need these capabilities." Here's where our interpersonal skills come into play. Without insulting him, we need to educate him, indicating that there may be other options that he isn't aware of.

"Clients don't know what they want," should not be a myth but an opportunity.

Myth #2. Even If Clients Know What They Want, It'll Take Weeks Or Maybe Months To Research and Discover Their True Needs.

Assume that the client has a good understanding of what she wants. This myth says there's a huge gap between wants and needs. The client can state wants in business terms, then it's up to us to translate into technical needs that we can deliver. Be systematic. I.S. should have a set procedure for analyzing each problem, a series of steps to follow with the client. If we're haphazard in our approach, the process can be lengthy. If we procrastinate—and often this myth is little more than an excuse to put the preliminary analysis off—then of course the time will whiz by.

This myth can also be an excuse for us to avoid the people side of the problem and head straight to the technical. "Research" will take a long time. Much of the preliminary research is understanding the business and people issues that contribute to the problem. If we're more comfortable dealing with the technical side, then it's natural to want to put off or minimize the importance of the "softer" issues. Fight against that urge. We must be well-rounded professionals who evaluate all parts of a problem.

Myth #3. If My Clients Aren't Satisfied With My Service, Typically It's Someone Else's Fault. It May Be The Client Himself, Other IPPs, Or Management.

This must stand out to every reader as passing the buck. Can anyone, reasonably say, I'm the only one here who's close to perfect. Look closely at where you want to lay the blame and trace the actions that led to that problem. How could it have gone otherwise? What could YOU have done differently?

We, as I.S. professionals, also tend to take things personally and be a bit too defensive. We're proud of our work, and if someone attacks it, our initial reaction may be hostile. "Don't tell me that's spaghetti code. It's structured code—my way." If we are to be a service organization, we need to relax a bit more.

Myth #4. Clients Are Irrational and Make It Impossible For Us To Keep Them Happy.

Excuses, excuses. This feeling may have any of three causes:

a. Some may think I.S. is naturally superior, more important, than other departments.

When we don't understand the processes needed to complete work in other departments, it's easy to think our department is more important. Or maybe it's just our natural egos at work. But I've seen many cases where lack of understanding of another department's work creates feelings of distrust because, however much we want to deny it, we just don't think they're as valuable to the company. If we do our preliminary research into the human and business aspects of each problem, we'll soon begin to see the other organization as a more unified whole, and see the need for each cog in the wheel.

b. We may think that most clients are inherently, ah, not very sharp.

This may be our mistaking lack of knowledge for stupidity. A stupid person lacks intelligence; an ignorant person doesn't have the facts. There's no problem being ignorant when it's not your area of expertise. A client doesn't need to know all about information systems. Part of your job is to create interfaces and provide training so that the client is protected from all the bits and bytes. Don't be upset or surprised when the client knows even less than you expect. When your knowledge is extensive, it's customary to overestimate what someone else, even someone you know is in another field, will understand about your work.

We may also think clients are difficult because they change their minds. This may be our fault. If we've been educating the client about the potential of computers, then the client naturally gets new, and maybe even better, ideas. In any event we must always be conscious of the fact that "we never embarrass our client."

c. We are covering up for our own inadequacies.

We may simply not want to face our own problems. It's easy to convince ourselves that someone else is the problem. It's hard to look objectively with ourselves in the middle of the picture and ask ourselves, "What's wrong with this picture?" Yet that objectivity is what's required if I.S. is to become a service organization.

Myth #5. Client Service Will Only Increase My Workload and Clients Don't Even Appreciate It.

We've seen that most people don't complain when something goes wrong, at least not to the person who needs to hear it. Even fewer people will give praise directly to the person who deserves it. And everyone needs to hear it.

A question here may well be, will client service increase our workload? More likely it'll increase our upfront expenditure of time, but reduce the problems encountered later in the project. And increase the agreeability of people we're working with, thereby reducing our headaches and stress.

"They just assume I'll drop everything when they call." This is tricky. Very often they call because there's a problem that's keeping them from doing their job. Naturally, they may panic. Here come the people skills again. We need to understand quickly the scope of the problem and prioritize. Then, in straightforward terms that don't leave your client in the dark, explain how we think the problem should be addressed. Don't be upset if they expect us to come running. They see us as a service organization and, in times of stress, may not recognize our work load.

Here's another way the clients, supposedly, don't appreciate our extra work. "No matter how hard I try, clients never build loyalty to I.S."

Loyalty is something people quietly practice. They don't go about singing their loyalties (except at the beginnings of ball games or on bumper stickers). Loyalty should be to the organization, anyway—an organization in which I.S. plays a major role.

Another complaint. "Clients never go to bat for us at budget time." How many other departments do we "go to bat for" at budget time?

Myth #6. I.S. is Too Large and Too Far Gone To Change Now.

This is no more than an excuse for inaction. Sure, it's harder to make a change when the organization is big and our business practices are ingrained, but when change is a necessity to remain competitive we meet our obstacles head-on.

Myth #7. Senior I.S. Management Will Soon Lose Interest.

This complaint is often based on experience. Unfortunately, service can be seen as "just the latest management phase. It'll pass, like all the rest." But this isn't like "the rest." If our companies aren't already working hard to improve client service, then we will soon be losing clients to competitors who are. If we ever allow it to get to this point, reversing it is impossible.

Myth #8. I.S. Service Costs Too Much.

The costs of quality service are a major field of study. Unfortunately, it's also imprecise because a major factor in calculating such quality costs is how much revenue or productivity is currently being lost by following present procedures. Equally hard to estimate is the payback from your new investment in service. Remember that service can be free in most instances, but building a truly functional service organization will incur cost. If you plan to do your own feasibility study, be sure to work the following cost items into your calculations:

- Cost of additional training (service skills)
- Cost of additional front end time (strategy development and research)

- Cost currently being lost in unnecessary questions and maintenance
- Cost currently being lost from mid-course corrections due to miscommunication
- Cost currently being lost from lack of repeat business
- Cost gained from future repeat business

This brief list is just intended to indicate the complexity of such calculations. To be accurate, I.S. also needs to figure in what effect improved I.S. service will have on the entire organization, not only on your department.

When people properly analyze their current situations, plan their implementation of improved service, and follow through on those plans, overall costs are saved while efficiency and productivity are improved.

Myth #9. Even If We Had the Money, We Don't Have the Time.

As with Myth #8, if we don't take the time now, we may soon have all the time in the world.

Myth #10. Achieving I.S. Client Satisfaction Can Be a Quick Fix.

The right consulting skills requires a balancing act between the quick fix and solutions to long-range problems.

Here's a situation that indicates the balancing that must be done. A colleague in a division of a major automotive company sought help from a well-known advanced technology consulting company. A senior representative from the consulting firm came and listened to the problems. As part of the explanation, my colleague was careful to explain the immediate needs. The consultant analyzed the situation and said that the problem was very deep. It would require about a year of work at a fee of about $500,000. The consultant's analysis paid no heed to the immediate needs.

There was nothing inaccurate in the consultant's analysis, but it showed no sensitivity to the stated needs. The consultant thought he knew better than those who had the problem. He didn't get the business. If the consultant had recommended a quick fix to take care of the immediate needs, but only on the condition that there was follow-up work to alleviate the underlying reason for the problem, then he probably would have received the assignment and been able to fix both their short- and long-range problems.

A client may be happy with a quick fix, but for how long? Our job is to listen to the problem, analyze it, and blend the client's professed needs with our deeper understanding of the technology. "Quick fix" implies rushed or incomplete. Sometimes a job can be completed quickly, but speed is not the ultimate goal. The goal is a satisfied, long-term client.

Myth #11. The Chances for Success are Pretty Low—
So Why Even Try?

You're right! If that's the attitude we begin with, our chances for success are pretty low. However, if a careful analysis shows that the chance of success really is low, then that affects our priorities and our advice as we discuss the options with our client. Be realistic and be honest.

Myth #12. Life Would Be Better Without Clients.

Ah, yes, we do all have tough clients, don't we? But we wouldn't have any work without clients. A friend of mine told me that he changed jobs three times and, poor man, his tough clients followed him every time! If we properly focus on client service, we're likely to find that many of our clients aren't as tough as we thought. As stated in my previous book *How To Market the I/S Department Internally*, we must realize that our clients are our only real reason for existence.

Ending the Myths

Every one of these myths has a basis in reality. But living by these myths is living in an unreal, negatively-viewed world that will only continue to get worse. Yes, clients are far from perfect. Change takes careful planning and time, and time is valuable. Which scenario, though, provides the greater risks?

1. Following the traditional guru-oriented approach, or
2. Providing the highest quality service that we can.

Nine Service Sins

Let's have a little fun. We've looked at a range of myths, and it's likely that part of you wants to believe in several of them. And even if you're able to see the error in them all, then you can still find someone else who works as if he lives by the myths. I'd like to categorize these myth mongers, these service sinners who prevent us from attaining a good service level. Can you think of anyone (include yourself) who sometimes falls into any of these categories? Better not write the names in this book. Then you won't be able to lend it to anyone. Or, better yet, write the names in. Then, when you recommend this book, they'll have to buy their own copies.

1. *The Dilligad:* This sounds like a creature Bilbo Baggins meets in some dark, dank cave. And the person who is a Dilligad bears a strong resemblance to such a demon. Dilligad stands for "Do I Look Like I Give a Darn?" How many times have you been a DILLIGAD? Remember it's estimated that 93% of our communication comes from non-verbals.

2. *The Ignorer:* "If I don't look at them maybe they'll go away." Have you ever wondered why some people rarely acknowledge you when you pass in the hall? Or why some people will end a discussion by simply starting to do something else? Are they just shy, uncomfortable in social situations, or are they full believers in the philosophy of The Ignorer?

3. *The Icicle:* Being The Icicle keeps people away from your door. If you give people a chilly reception and project a profound impatience that shouts out, "Get the message? Go away!," you won't see clients unless they have an emergency.

4. *The Patronizer:* Using computerese makes you sound so impressive. You sure know your stuff. But your client is left feeling intimidated, confused, and, quite possibly, humiliated. In effect, you've said to your client, "Gee, this is awfully complicated and you probably won't understand it." As I've said before, you should avoid technical jargon and your client should avoid jargon from his business area. If, however, jargon is simply the most precise, accurate means of expression, clearly define the term.

5. *The Otto Matic:* Can you think of any mechanical responses that you give to certain situations? Things you say without thinking, and without sincerity? How many do you hear from other people, when you're the customer or the client?

> "Thank you, have a nice day."
> "It's been a pleasure serving you."
> "Come again."
> "Sorry, but I don't . . ."
> "No, we can't do that."
> "If you'll come back on . . ."

Probably the leading mechanical response Otto gives is "Hi, how are ya?" or "How ya doin." This is usually said in passing or in greeting. If said in passing, how often do you think Otto wants a serious answer. He's probably ten feet down the corridor before you respond. If said in greeting, try giving full, honest responses for a while and see how people will react. In short, be sincere and treat each individual as a valued client.

6. *The Rule Master:* "It's company policy . . ." Many, many people find policy easy to hide behind. The implication is that "I'm a nice person, but the organization has these rules that I have to follow. Now, if it were my way . . ." An additional problem is people are often instructed to hide behind rules. They have no empowerment to solve anything but the most direct problems, leaving them no recourse but to spout policy.

7. *The Great Evader:* The Great Evader is a first cousin to The Rule Master. You won't find either of them taking a hard look at a problem. The Great Evader avoids taking responsibility (again, lack of empowerment can be a contributing factor). A typical response might be, "The person you need is . . ." or "We don't handle that, you want . . ."

8. *The X.Q.Ser:* The problem is with the client or the "system" or management. Excuses and explanation come in a never-ending stream. And have you noticed how, when you can show the X.Q.Ser that she made an error or that he can handle the problem, there's rarely an apology and acceptance of responsibility?

9. *The UNderdog:* An underdog is expected to lose, but usually will still try hard. Within a service environment, The UNderdog projects defeat almost with every action.

UNenthusiastic	UNtouched
UNexcited	UNinterested
UNambitious	UNmoved
UNimpassioned	UNfriendly
UNinspired	UNaware

Have you caught on that such an attitude is UNnecessary and contrary to a good service attitude?

PERSONAL ACTION PLAN

Worksheet

MYTHS AND SINS

Specific ideas I can use on the job:

Specific actions I will take within 30 days:

Chapter 7
Moments of Truth

"Your first appearance is the gauge by which you will be measured; try to manage that you may go beyond yourself in after times, but beware of ever doing less."

—Jean Jacques Rousseau

Definition

Earlier, we determined that moments of truth are the microorganisms that make up service. Moments of truth is the phrase I prefer for any occurrence in which the client comes into contact with any aspect of our organization and gets an impression of the quality of our service. The phrase "Moments of Truth" was coined by Jan Carlzon, the President of Scandinavian Airline Systems (SAS). A good definition was created by Albrecht and Bradford in *Service America*.

A Moment of Truth (MOTs) is that precise instant when the customer comes into contact with any aspect of your business and, on the basis of that contact, forms an opinion about the quality of your service and, potentially, the quality of your product.

From these Moments of Truth client expectations are set. Moments of Truth:

■ Are the basic building blocks of service.
■ Are the smallest indivisible unit.
■ Form the basis for service.

> *"Moments of Truth" is the phrase I prefer for any occurrence in which the client comes into contact with any aspect of our organization and gets an impression of the quality of our service.*

Before, we've mostly been discussing the goals of service. We want to manage client expectations so that we achieve client satisfaction. Now we'll get into the process. Awareness is the first step. Once we understand when and how Moments of Truth occur, we can start to make use of them.

You may be thinking, "Hey, wait a minute! You're saying that my client's impression is being formed every time he's in contact with us, or hears something about us, or thinks of us while using our services or applications. Moments of Truth are never ending."

That's right. And we can never stop being vigilant about the Moment of Truth.

Using Moments of Truth

There are a number of things we can do to ensure positive, productive Moments of Truth.

- Start thinking in terms of outcomes
- Inventory the Moments of Truth our client experiences
- Analyze each Moment of Truth from the standpoint of quality
- Look for ways to improve and add value.

Outcomes

Let's take these one at a time. First, start thinking in terms of outcomes. Most people don't consciously think of how their reactions or words will affect other people; they just say and do what comes naturally. And most people are naturally a bit self-centered.

Think of any recent meeting you've had with a client. What had an influence on the way the client perceives you or your department? Make a list. Every item on that list indicates a moment of truth, maybe several of them. Just take a minute to do this, then go on to the next page.

Here are a few of the items you may have listed:

> What client had been told by others
> My appearance
> Location of meeting
> My greeting
> How I sat
> How concerned I was with the problem
> How well I listened
> How well I understood
> What questions I asked
> How knowledgeable I was:
>> About client's department
>> About client's problem
>> About client's system
>> About possible solutions

Clearly, this list can go on and on.

A Model to Examine

Now, so that we can all consider the same example, let's consider restaurants. What kind of service do you expect? Besides "good service," you probably immediately need to know what kind of restaurant we're discussing. You don't expect the same service from a gourmet French restaurant that you expect from a fast-food place, yet each can give you outstanding service. Your perception is colored by your expectations.

McDonald's prides itself on outstanding service, and most people seem to agree, so let's examine how they do it.

Moments of Truth

On Figure 7-1, list Moments of Truth (MOTs) for McDonald's. So that we all start from the same concept, imagine that you're driving along the highway after dark looking for a place to eat. Right down the MOTs on the form as they come up. A sign on the side of the road indicates gas, lodging and a McDonald's at the next exit. What's the first Moment of Truth? Let's walk through this together for a while.

As you get off the highway, is it clear which direction you turn to get to the restaurant? If not, you might get right back on the highway, rather than risk driving in the wrong direction. Let's say there is a sign and you turn right. The next Moment of Truth may be the location. If you've driven two miles and still haven't arrived, you may turn back. But there it is. What may be the next MOT? The first thing you see is the sign or perhaps the Golden Arches. Are they clearly visible or hidden by trees? Are all the letters lit? Is everything bright and clean? If not, you might make a judgment to look for another restaurant.

If the lights pass the test, you next approach the parking lot. Is it full or empty? Depending on your mood, either answer could bring you in or send you away. If no one is there, you may think the food or service is poor, so turn away; or maybe you're pleased because there are no lines, so you go in. If the lot is overflowing, the lines might turn you away, or you might assume that a crowd means the food or service is outstanding and so you turn in. As you see how a Moment of Truth can so easily be either positive or negative, you see how tricky the right decision or action may be, and how much sensitivity to your customers is needed.

Now, fill out the rest of your trip to McDonald's on the Critical Moments of Truth. You've probably gathered that every MOT is critical, so be picky. Don't forget such MOTs as who's loitering in the shadows of the parking lot, and whether your feet stick to the entryway floor, and whether the door handle is grungy, and whether your soft drink is 90% ice. (How easily negative MOTs come to mind.) Another debatable MOT is how many burgers are sitting under that yellow light? If it's during rush hour, you know they haven't been there long, so if there are many it means your order will be filled quickly. If it's 10 p.m. and there are many of them, you'll figure that they've been sitting there for a while, so the immediacy of service isn't as important as how recently they were prepared.

A Process Divided

Now take your MOTs and see if there are natural divisions into sections. I suggest that there are. There are three natural divisions: Entry, Process, and Exit. Everything that occurs at McDonald's before you get into line is part of the Entry. While the entire list is a continuous process, the "Process" that stands out is the making, delivery, and consuming of the product, so the Process runs from placing

Figure 7-1. Critical Moments of Truth Analysis

CUSTOMER   McDONALD'S

Entry Phase

Process Phase

Exit Phase

_____ % Satisfaction   _____ % Satisfaction

your order to finding your seat and eating. Once you finish your Big Mac, the Exit begins.

How perfect can McDonald's, or any fast food chain, expect to be in meeting its MOT? Obviously, you'd like to be at 100% customer satisfaction, and you can aim for it, but priorities are going to enter into your maintenance, upkeep, and training. Employees can always aim for and expect 100%, but you, as manager, will have to make choices. You'll have to place some things above others in importance. Let's assume that this restaurant says it will be at peak functioning if it meets or exceeds expectations for 95% of the MOT.

This is a business decision. The manager will be happy if the MOT are satisfied at 95% efficiency 100% of the time.

Where can you, as the manager, most easily accept that 5% loss. Is it while the customer is deciding whether or not to enter? (Entry) Is it during the process of interaction with the salesperson? (Process) Is it as the customer exits? (Exit)

Most people say that most or all of that 5% loss is best if it comes at the Exit. First, you've got to bring the customer in, then the service and eating comprise the most memorable part. If the customer is pleased with all that, she's not going to be overly upset if the trash bins are too full. Or is she?

Using this example see if you can fill in the MOT's that clients face during a routine stop at McDonalds. Use form 7-1. If you were the manager where would you (what phase) be willing to give up 5%?

An I.S. Inventory

What you've just been doing is creating an inventory of Moments of Truth. Now let's make it job-related, moving from the example you just used to a corporate situation. First, choose a department within I.S. or a service that I.S. performs. Now go through the same procedure as before. Start from the moment someone calls (or looks for your phone number). Use the space in Figure 7-2 to list the points at which the client forms a perception of the quality of your service. And use your client's eyes. How easy is it for someone to reach us, then to reach the right person? How easy is it to put the request forward? How was the priority of this project determined? How quick is our response time? No excuses. No rationalizations. Just the facts. Use

Figure 7-2. I.S. Moments of Truth

I.S.	To be used as examples only
Entry Phase	Enter MOT activities that your client must go through in the entry phase of working with you. Greeting, phone answering, responsiveness of staff, clean office, etc.
Process Phase	Enter MOT activities that your clients see during the process phase of working with you. Knowledge level of staff, responsiveness, red tape, signature level for approval, etc.
Exit Phase	Enter MOT activities that apply when you conclude the client interaction. Problems answered, plan for follow through established, etc.
____ % Satisfaction	What % of satisfaction are you ready to accept?

the divisions to indicate where the Entry ends and Process begins, and then where the Process ends and Exit begins.

Were you easily able to determine the dividing points? What is the current percentage of expectation fulfillment in each section? How acceptable are those percentages? What is a realistic target percentage for fulfillment in each section? How can you improve the percentages? Your answers to these questions, if you were working in a group, will take hours, perhaps days, and will lead to primary improvement activities.

It's likely that you'll find yourself weakest in the Entry and Exit areas. These are the ones emphasizing people skills and non-technical work. The Process is probably your strongest feature. Typically the Entry and the Exit are where the most work is needed.

Reputation, Reputation, Reputation

At one point in Shakespeare's *Othello*, Iago says, "Reputation, reputation, reputation. I have lost the immortal part of myself and what remains is bestial." Iago believes that his reputation will remain longer than he will, much longer than the facts that led to that reputation. And they will. Your clients will pass on anything about you that makes the best conversation, and more often than not, they'll talk about mistakes. Minimize mistakes and you'll emphasize the positive as clients build your reputation.

Every Moment of Truth is important. Whether good or bad, it can have a snowball effect. Going out of your way once to help someone in another department may spread throughout the organization so that people who don't know you may see you as a saint.

A Collective Inventory

Work with your colleagues to develop an inventory for at least one aspect of your organization. Use flip charts to record your listing. Now deal with the same questions that you dealt with when working alone. Mark where the Entry ends and Process begins, and then where the Process ends and Exit begins. What is the current percentage of expectation fulfillment in each section? How acceptable are those percentages? What is a realistic target percentage for fulfillment in each section? How can you improve the percentages?

I'm confident that IPPs are already doing fine work in the Process portion. We know how to do "our job" well, but now that our job has expanded, we need to concentrate on the Entry and the Exit while maintaining our high standards for the process.

PERSONAL ACTION PLAN

Worksheet

MOMENTS OF TRUTH

Specific ideas I can use on the job:

Specific actions I will take within 30 days:

Chapter 8

Learning About Your Clients

"All persons are puzzles until at last we find in some word or act the key to the man, the woman; straightaway all their past words and actions lie in light before us."

—*Ralph Waldo Emerson*

Ways to Learn

> ## "There is no substitute for knowing your client."

By now, that point is clear, but for a concept this important, repetition doesn't hurt.

How do you learn about your clients? Much of it comes naturally out of conversation, but you can serve your clients better if you consciously use specific tools and techniques and keep careful records. People in your department change, and new personnel need to review the records of your existing and prospective clients. I divide those records, information, into three types:

- Quantitative
- Qualitative
- Front Line

Quantitative Information

Quantitative information is usually in the form of statistics about large numbers of people. 32% of American homes have a personal computer. 73% of businesses and 4% of homes have a fax machine. The average American between the ages of 12–18 watches 3.2 hours of television per day. These statistics (which I made up) are all quantitative. Four tools are common for gathering sizeable quantities of information.

- Existing demographic studies
- Survey questionnaires
- Reaction cards
- Pre- and post-inquiries

Demographic study results can be found in such places as the annual *Information Please Almanac* and *American Demographics* magazine. If you require relatively general information about large numbers of the population, then that information likely exists and you'll save considerable research time by finding it before you begin your own surveys. This is most likely to be necessary if many of your clients come from outside your organization.

More specific, targeted information can be obtained using your own marketing department or a professional research firm. Both will research what you need by creating a customized survey. Everyone is familiar with surveys, but a marketing professional should design the survey because, as with focus groups, it's hard to ask a series of simple question that don't lead readers toward any answers. These surveys may be distributed by mail, or given by telephone, or perhaps you'll set up a table by the exit from the company cafeteria.

Reaction cards are filled out right after a service or a meeting. Pointed questions are asked about the quality, convenience, and needs of the customer. For example, many restaurants will have cards on the table for you to evaluate the quality of the food and the service. Reaction cards are on-the-spot evaluations. We call reaction cards "quantitative information," but if you work in a small operation, you'll collect relatively few cards. However, it may still be the majority of the people receiving a particular service who respond; that's why we call it quantitative.

Pre- and post-inquiries are surveys used before and after some work with the client. First, they measure what the client's expectations are; afterwards they record how well those expectations were fulfilled. Often you'll find cards packaged with products you buy. The questions may be attached to the warranty in an effort to get a higher rate of return. These can be viewed as either pre-inquiries because they're before the use of the product, or post-inquiries because they're after the sale. It all depends on your purpose for the survey.

As with reaction cards, you may be collecting relatively few cards, but over time the numbers build up, showing trends in client needs and attitudes which you need to monitor consistently.

What is Qualitative Information?

Qualitative information will help you determine how to position your product or services. In our case, the product is service. But before we discuss I.S., let's look at more typical cases. Let me ask you, do you place more value on a product if it's:

> Expensive
> Advertised in magazines or newspapers that you read
> Advertised during specific TV programs
> Sold in certain stores and not in others
> Promoted by a major sports figure
> Promoted by a rock star
> Promoted by a symphony conductor
> Promoted by a business leader
> Wearing the "Good Housekeeping Seal of Approval"

This is information that is usually gleaned from the quantitative information, enhanced by more directed questions. If 78% of our prospective audience is male, between the ages of 18–45, and 84% of that audience watches at least three sporting events a week, then we might infer that Roger Clemens could help us sell our product more effectively than could Danielle Steele.

Let's turn this information to our own advantage. Remember the five evaluation categories: Responsiveness, Assurance, Tangibles, Reliability, and Empathy. We need to understand not only that all of them are important, but which is more important in particular circumstances. As a manager, you may have determined that 92% effectiveness in meeting Moments of Truth is a figure you can be happy with. By understanding your clients, you can determine where that 8% can be lost with the least negative effect.

> *Face-to-face interviews can be the most time-consuming, but also the most precise.*

Qualitative Information Gathering

Qualitative information is more personal than quantitative, and it needs to be designed by you or a marketing department or advertising group so that it's tailored to your particular needs. There are six main techniques for gathering qualitative information:

- User groups
- Professional associations
- Face-to-face interviews
- Focus groups
- Follow-up telephone and written surveys
- Opportunistic interviews

I place user groups and professional associations first because they're straddling the definitions of quantitative and qualitative. If your clients are members of a particular user group or professional association, you can get information about the group's membership. If the group is sufficiently small and targeted, if it's composed entirely of your client base, then it's a good source for qualitative information. But if the group is an electrical engineering association and you have a number of electrical engineers among your clients, the information will be too diffuse, representative of too large a body to be effective for qualitative information.

Face-to-face interviews can be the most time-consuming, but also the most precise. They allow you to probe for whatever details you need. Just be sure to weigh the importance and the nature of the information you need, and don't use valuable time for individual meetings if the material can just as well be gathered in other ways.

In a focus group, you assemble a small number, usually 5–10, representative people who can give the information you need. Whenever possible, select people who give you a diversity of opinion, and whose opinions you already respect. A focus group usually functions best when led by an experienced facilitator. The leader must avoid leading questions that indicates what answer is desired—and that's not easy to do if you're involved in the decision-making process.

If these techniques don't turn up enough information, then use follow-up telephone or written surveys. You'll often have to return to a source to get specific details, or to ask a question that arose when you were analyzing the data you collected.

Lastly, take advantage of opportunistic interviews. An unplanned meeting can often yield a more relaxed, informal conversation. You're not likely to be planning questions for unplanned meetings, but if you're ever-alert to client needs, you'll find the right questions will just flow when you get a comfortable moment with a client.

When there are a variety of techniques to choose from, it's important to weigh the pros and cons of each in deciding which is appropriate. Just what do you need to learn? Do you need a great deal of information or the answer to a limited question? How much time do you have? Will a few well-chosen interviewees be representative? Will people be more open or honest in a face-to-face meeting than if responding by telephone or mail? Will people be swayed by others in a focus group?

Front Line Reports

These are reports by people in your group who work with the client. Members of your group can report on such things as the details of what's going on inside the operation, or report on warning signs where potential difficulties may be brewing. They can also ask direct questions. This isn't the same as face-to-face interviews because the interviews are formal situations. Here it's just asking a pointed question of one client with whom you work. Such questions might include:

- How satisfied were you with our service?
- Was there anything that caused a problem for you?
- Is there any message you would like to pass on to our management?
- What could we have done better in serving you?
- Did you get the help you needed?

As you and others in your group work with clients, your ears are open. You hear things that may or may not get passed on. If they do get passed on, it may only be at the status of rumor. You should formalize the reporting process enough so that management hears about both strengths and weaknesses, but this must be done in a way that doesn't become obtrusive.

Department Profile

Following are three sample forms that you're welcome to use, either directly as they are or to adapt if you have additional or different needs. First is a Departmental Client Profile, second is an Individual Client Profile, and third is a Contact Information.

The Departmental Profile, shown in Figure 8-1, records key facts about your client's department. It's brief, providing a quick overview for anyone in I.S. who wants to make a strong connection and remember important names, numbers, reporting relationships, and your past work history with the department.

Figure 8-1. Departmental Client Profile

1. Dept. Name _____

2. Location _____

3. Responsibilities of Dept. _____

4. Reporting Structure _____
   Director_____
   General Manager _____
   (fill in titles) _____

5. Departmental telephone _____

6. Departmental secretary _____
   telephone _____
   E-mail _____
   fax _____

7. Key telephone & fax numbers & E-mail addresses

8. Past Service History for each project, record the following:

   Dept. Coordinator _____ I.S. Coordinator_____
   Description of Project_____

   Date Begun _____
   Milestones _____
   _____

   Date Completed _____
   Maintenance History _____
   _____
   _____

   Comments _____
   _____
   _____
   _____

Individual Client Profile

Our Individual Client Profile is adapted from a similar profile used by the MacKay Envelope Company. There's nothing wrong with borrowing ideas from companies that have done things well. It's important for us to avoid adopting an NIH attitude. If we believe something that's "Not Invented Here" can't be of use because we need everything tailored exactly to our specifications, from scratch, then we're wasting a lot of time. We should keep our eyes open for techniques others are using. This is the informal side of benchmarking.

The Individual Client Profile, Figure 8-2, is a list of 58 facts that create a detailed record of an individual client. There's probably a lot more detail here than you have in your current records on clients, but you never know when a particular fact will help you understand your clients needs or attitudes better, or help you through a rough spot in a discussion or negotiation. Naturally, these are not all questions you're likely to just ask. Many of these will come out over time in conversation. If the "fact" being recorded is really an opinion or an impression, the name of the person recording the information and the date should be appended to the info on that line. In this way, a query can easily be raised if someone else learns contradictory facts.

Much of this can simply be looked at as reminders. The facts may be those you'd really like to remember, but they're just not quite important enough to stick. If you care about your client, there's genuine interest when you say, "I recall that your daughter just began college. How's she doing," or "So, how did you enjoy the Caribbean." Yet they're both details you're likely to forget if they're not written down.

Some of these may seem too personal at first glance, but they can help you make your client feel at ease. You might ask yourself, "What do I care what my client likes to eat or drink? But if it's a client who you may occasionally go out to dinner with, and he usually enjoys a particular type of food or drink, it can only help you if you remember.

This form has a place to indicate when and by whom it was last updated. This is for significant updates, not just adding or changing a line, which should be noted on that line.

Maintaining such an Individual Client Profile Sheet becomes a matter of habit. After a conversation, get used to jotting down whatever new, pertinent information you've learned.

It should be noted, however, that some companies have strict policies regarding the collection of data on employees. While none of the information gathered with the Client Profile Sheet is meant to do any more than provide further understanding of your client, check your company's policy about such practices prior to beginning your work in the area.

Figure 8-2. Client Profile Sheet

Date _____

Last updated _____

By _____

CLIENT

1. Name _____
   Nickname _____
   Pronunciation _____
   Title _____

2. Division/Location _____

3. Telephone—Business _____
   FAX _____

4. Birth date and place _____
   Hometown _____

5. Outstanding physical characteristics (Examples: great condition, arthritis, severe back problems, diet) _____
   _____

EDUCATION

6. High school and year _____
   College _____
   Graduated when _____
   Degrees _____

7. College honors _____
   Advanced degrees _____

8. College fraternity or sorority _____
   Sports _____

9. Extracurricular college activities _____
   _____

Figure 8-2. *(continued)*

10. Military service _____
    Discharge rank _____
    Years of service _____

FAMILY

11. Marital status _____
    Spouse's name _____

12. Spouse's education _____

13. Spouse's interests/activities/affiliations _____
    _____

14. Wedding anniversary _____

15. Children, if any, names and ages _____
    _____

16. Children's education _____

17. Children's interests (hobbies, problems, etc.) _____
    _____

BUSINESS BACKGROUND

18. Previous employment: (most recent first)
    Company _____
    Location _____
    Date(s) _____
    Title(s) _____

    Company _____
    Location _____
    Date(s) _____
    Title(s) _____

19. Previous position at present company _____
    _____
    _____
    Title(s) _____
    Date(s) _____

20. Any "status" symbols in office? _____

21. Professional or trade associations _____
    _____
    Office or honors in them _____

22. What adjectives would you use to describe client? _____
_____

23. What is he/she most proud of having achieved? _____
_____

24. Any mentors? _____

25. What business relationship does he/she have with I.S.? _____
_____

26. Is it a good relationship? _____
What makes it so? _____
_____

GOALS

27. What is his/her immediate business objective? _____
_____

28. What is his/her long-range business objective? _____
_____

SPECIAL INTERESTS

29. Clubs or service clubs (Masons, Kiwanis, Country Club, etc.) _____
_____

30. Active in community? _____
How? _____

LIFE STYLE

31. Favorite place for lunch _____
Dinner _____

32. Favorite items on menu _____

33. Does client object to having anyone buy his/her meal?
_____

34. Hobbies and recreational interests _____
_____
What does the client like to read? _____
_____

35. Vacation habits _____
_____

Figure 8-2. *(continued)*

36. Spectator-sports interest: sports and teams _____
_____

37. Kind of car(s) _____

38. Conversational interests _____
_____

THE CLIENT AND YOU

39. Does the proposal you plan to make to him/her require
client to change a habit or take an action that is contrary
to custom? _____

40. Is he/she primarily concerned about the opinion of others?
_____

41. What are the key problems as the client sees them? _____
_____

42. What are the priorities of the client's management? _____

Any conflicts between client and management? _____
_____

43. Can you help with these problems? _____
How? _____
_____

44. Does your competitor have better answers to the above
questions than you have? _____
_____

ADDITIONAL NOTES

Adapted from: MacKay Envelope Corp.

We suggest that the Profile Sheets should be kept by the I.S. secretary or office administrator and the information on individuals should be accessible only to individuals working directly with the client. The Departmental Profiles should be available to anyone in I.S. Some I.S. organizations allow access electronically and provide a client profile screen as you work with the particular client.

Contact Information

As an individual, you may want to keep your own abbreviated version of the Individual Client Profile for those with whom you're directly. Working with a sample of what this form may look like is in Figure 8-3, Contact Information.

Figure 8-3.   Sample Contact Information

CLIENT PROFILE (Abbreviated Version)

DATE:_____ REVISED: _____

Name: _____

Title:_____

Address: _____

_____

Phone: _____

FAX: _____

Where/When

   Met: _____

_____

Names

   Family:_____

_____

Associates: _____

_____

Dates
  Birthday: _____
  Anniversary: _____

Hobbies/Interests: _____

_____

_____

Education: _____

_____

Places Lived: _____

_____

Specialization: _____

_____

Dislikes: _____

_____

_____

Current Work: _____

_____

_____

Previous Work: _____

_____

_____

Figure 8-3. Sample Contact Information *(continued)*

Short-term Goals: _____

_____

Long-term Goals: _____

_____

Current Concerns: _____

_____

Conversation Log

Most of the Sample Conversation Log, Figure 8-4, is self-explanatory. This helps you keep track of both telephone and personal contact with your client. The final column, containing both a dollar sign and "Time," provides a place to record your billable hours. If you're working on a fee basis, you should still keep track of how long you spend with a client. This provides valuable information for determining how appropriate your rates are. There's another way this column might be used, to. Record any unofficial estimates you give your client about time or expenses involved in different aspects of the project. You may want a log with separate columns for remembering conversational estimates and recording billable hours. The important thing is not that you use our form, but that you keep an ongoing log, and tailor it to your specific needs.

As stated earlier, all of these Profiles and Logs can easily be recorded on a computer, which may make updating easier. However, if placed on a network, you need to carefully consider who requires access to which forms.

Figure 8-4. Sample Conversation Log

WAYS TO LEARN ABOUT YOUR CLIENT

Client: _____

Time/ Date	Discussed, Requested, Promised	Dates of Follow-Up	$ Time

PERSONAL ACTION PLAN

Worksheet

LEARNING ABOUT YOUR CLIENTS

Specific ideas I can use on the job:

Specific actions I will take within 30 days:

Chapter 9

Developing Your Service Strategy

"Managing in accordance with a strategic plan is a learned art. The longer you use the tool, the better you are able to manage with it."
—R. Henry Miglione

To Read Or . . .

Reading this chapter is optional. If your place in the organization means that you won't be involved in developing the I.S. service strategy, you might skip to Chapter 10. Then again, if you read this chapter, you may be able to make some valuable suggestions to management. All I need to say here is that this chapter is primarily for management who'll be determining and implementing a service strategy.

As you read through this chapter and begin to plan your service strategy or check your current service strategy against my suggestions, you'll find a number of concepts that recur in different guises. This is an intentional built-in redundancy that forces you to continue looking at the most important elements. It also reminds you that your service process is always ongoing, is always being reevaluated.

The Benefits

How formal is your strategy for providing good service? There are numerous reasons for formalizing your strategic plans. A Service Strategy therefore:

1. Identifies your clients. Sure, you know who your clients are now, but do you really understand how likely other prospective clients are to seek your help? With a formal service strategy, you're more likely to keep those you have, win new clients sooner, and satisfy them better. You'll be forced to know who you must satisfy and what they want from a relationship with I.S.

2. Determines how much your clients value various parts of your services and products. You learn if your emphases are placed properly. Which MOTs should you focus on? Where's the biggest payoff? Track any changes you make to demonstrate service gains or improvements.

3. Establishes your client's service expectations. A clear strategy lets your clients know what they can expect. This keeps expectations realistic.

4. Indicates how much you will have to spend to satisfy those expectations. Careful planning yields a more accurate budget forecast. It helps you determine needs in such areas as staffing, products, service delivery, and hours of operation.

5. Becomes a rallying point. It unifies IPPs around a common purpose. If you're all working under a common philosophy of purpose, it shows.

6. Identifies philosophical and operational conflicts with policy and standards. Of course, once you've identified such conflicts, then the real challenge begins—to bring policy or standards in line with the agreed-upon philosophy or method of operation.

7. Helps identify valid performance measurements. Thus begins the process of putting measurement tools in place. Monitoring your progress over time and analyzing trends allows you to measure the results of improvements.

8. Pays off in increased respect and revenue. If your service strategy yields the first seven benefits, then this one should follow automatically.

Developing the Strategy

Three key elements within each organization, shown in Figure 9-1, must be addressed and understood before you can successfully develop your service strategy. The goal here is not to try and change or try to implement a new corporate structure, but to try and understand it so we can respond with a service strategy that will be more in line with your corporation's expectations of your service.

Figure 9-1. Organizational Control

Management Philosophies
Managerial Style
Organizational Structure

Management Philosophies. What is the embedded philosophy within your corporation? Is management innovative? conservative? Understand your corporate environment. If you're not using an independent consultant to help with this analysis, be sure your readings and talks with those in other companies are broad enough so that you understand the wealth of philosophies that are possible. If you've lived with one management philosophy for years, it's sometimes hard to open your mind to other options.

Managerial Style. What style is currently in place? Is it dictatorial? Participative? Encouraging? Intimidating? Has the current management been in place long? Under the present style and philosophy has business been improving? declining? holding steady? Answers here will contribute to how you develop your strategy, how you implement it, and what it will include.

Organizational Structure. Where does I.S. fit in the overall structure of the corporation? Is there a CIO? Is someone from I.S. in the top level strategic planning group? Is I.S. an admired group? Respected? How well known are we?

Objectives

Once you define and understand the three key elements of your organizational structure, you will be prepared for the next step—to define your objectives and how they can successfully complement your corporation's organizational structure. I have identified these as eleven objectives.

1. Define your purpose in the workplace. What are your organization's objectives? Write a clear mission statement. Ask, "How do we look and fit within the overall corporate management philosophy?" It flushes out any misunderstandings in the wider, organizational perspective.

2. Define exactly who you are and who your clients are/should be. Do a detailed audience profile. The more you know about your client's wants, needs, management philosophy, etc. the better prepared you will be to adopt a service strategy that meets their expectations.

3. Define your value added contribution to the organization. Where would your services be found if you weren't around? Why can I.S. perform those services better than anyone else? What I.S. services can be performed as effectively by others? Should they be moved?

4. Define what you expect your client expectations to be. This involves analyzing what those expectations currently are and whether that differs from what they should be.

5. Define what will be an acceptable service level for your organization to meet or exceed. Look back to your earlier analysis of the MOT. Exactly what satisfaction percentage will you be able to live with on each level of the MOT.

6. Define your systems that will clearly measure your level of service. How will you ensure that you constantly meet client expectations?

7. Define the skills and resources required by the staff to meet or exceed the desired service level.

8. Define the mechanisms by which the staff will be trained to have the necessary skills. Will it be a minimum number of training hours per year? How might training be tied to your staff evaluation procedure?

9. Define the means by which the staff will have the necessary resources. Money, tools, space, time—how will you monitor appropriate resource levels?

10. Define a staff motivational reward structure. Do you want the structure to be only team-oriented, or to reward both teams and individuals? Simple recognition for a job well done is an outstanding motivator, yet one that's often overlooked by management. Just ask good performers if they feel as though they're sufficiently appreciated.

11. Define the procedure by which I.S. will market itself and its service policy to the rest of the organization. After all, you can't just sit back and wait for clients to come to you.

Guiding Questions

Defining the eleven objectives carries you a long way toward determining your service strategy. As you work on the definitions, many questions will arise. The following guiding questions are intended to give you a jump on some of the definitions, to help you anticipate items that will need to be addressed. These do not necessarily correlate in sequence to the eleven objectives, but rather as added-value for consideration.

1. Is your organization ready for measurements against a service level? Will your staff accept and take ownership for the new ideas and principles they'll be measured against? If not, why not? If yes, what type of measurement will be needed?

2. How will those who are to administer any operational changes view the new service level? Will it be looked upon as unwanted bureaucracy? Will it be a beneficial change desired to beat the competition? Will they think WIIFM? (What's in it for me?)

3. Do you have the resources you may need as an organization to implement a successful, ongoing service approach? In this case, "organization" applies at two levels: first to the larger company that you're a part of, and second to your own I.S. group.

4. Do you have a management philosophy that encourages and supports a high level of service participation, such as the 4 Cs of Support, which we discussed in Chapter 3?

Comfort	Confrontation
Clarification	Celebration

5. What are the written and unwritten rules by which your organization operates? This returns us to the Organizational Control listing in Figure 9-1. If you don't understand these rules, then the informal way can take over when you least expect it and undo everything you've done.

6. What are your CIO/management expectations? Do they have special interest areas? Are their service priorities aligned with yours? (Or are yours aligned with theirs?)

7. Are service teams of IPPs established to provide service for clients. Should they be? Should clients be visited or served in pairs? in teams? What are the advantages? Disadvantages? How much experience do you have working in teams? If you plan to develop teams, how much training is necessary for everyone to understand how to work on a team? To accept working on a team?

8. What are the strengths and weaknesses in the skills of your current staff? It's easy to concentrate on the weaknesses and focus training in those areas. But it's equally important to understand the strengths and perhaps build some of your early steps in the service strategy around the strengths.

> *Make it clear that you welcome input at all stages of the service strategy development, and will continue to welcome input after a strategy is in place.*

Involving the Staff

As you answer the above questions and strive for clear definition of all the objectives, it's important to involve those who'll eventually be implementing the strategy. Make it clear that you welcome input at all stages of the service strategy development, and will continue to welcome input after a strategy is in place. Be sure a simple procedure exists for staff feedback. But at the same time make it clear that final decisions reside with the management group who must ultimately answer to senior management.

Call for a participative meeting with IPPs and discuss:

- What is service?
- Why should we have a service strategy?
- Who are our clients?
- What is our current service vision, goals, objective, philosophy?
- How do clients view current I.S. service?
- Why should our clients choose us?
- Should we consider client incentives (like guaranteeing our work)?
- Who is our competition?
- What competitive advantages do we offer against our competition?
- Should our service goal be:
  - —To provide one-stop service?
  - —To be the computer technology provider of first choice?
  - —To be the best service provider in a certain line of business/technology?

The importance of agreeing on a definition of superior service cannot be overestimated. The same things must be important to everyone. What are the components of service? What must be done consistently to keep each component at a high service level?

When discussing our service strategy, explore both the benefits to us and to our clients if a service strategy is implemented.

Checks and Balances

To ensure client satisfaction, your service level must continuously exceed client expectations. Implementing a series of checks and balances will help you keep a watch on both client expectations and how they may be changing, as well as how you meet those evolving expectations. To help you with this, we have developed a five-step implementation procedure.

1. Identify what is of highest priority to your primary clients, those who consistently provide a high volume of business. Is it:
   - Timeliness
   - Consistency
   - Cost of service/product
   - Knowledgeable and receptive staff
   - Having a participative role in decision-making
   - Response time
   - Follow through

   All are important—you know that—but not all are of equal importance to each client. Once you understand the relative importance of these items, you need a mechanism to continually measure your effectiveness. The following is one way such a mechanism can be created.

2. Develop a simple client survey. The survey should measure how well you:
   - Have influenced clients' expectations
   - Meet clients' expectations
   - Meet clients' needs
   - Understand clients' service requirements

   The survey should be designed for both electronic and manual responses.

3. When the survey is first designed, test it on two or three willing clients who understand that it is a survey being beta tested. The clients should clearly know your philosophy and why you've created the test. Most likely the client has had a hand in the departmental changes you've been making, so the request for assistance won't come out of the blue.

   Whether or not the survey keeps the client anonymous depends on how the survey is to be used. If you're going to do a blanket survey all at once, then anonymity is usually desired. If you're administering the survey at the completion of each project, then naturally you'll know the client. Also consider whether you want the questions to refer to specific projects or if the questions should be more generic.

   If you do decide on generic questions and anonymous responses, you may want to embed codes to provide geographic locations or the size of the client organization or the frequency of I.S. service use. Such codes can simply be the same number printed on each survey that goes to the Northwest, or the same letter on each survey that's sent to engineering. Surveys will be anonymous for individuals, but still representative of a division or a region.

4. As the surveys are returned, measure them against expectations. For the beta test, you'll need to determine whether results that are far from your expectations are more due to the phrasing of the questions or inaccurate expectations. Enter the results of each survey in a data base, so you can track and compare the results of surveys given at different times. Look for gradual trends in the responses.

5. You now have a final survey form. If results from your "final" survey are considerably askew from your expectations, you'll likely need to adjust the way your service philosophy is being implemented. This may involve additional training or mentoring for members of your staff. Also, no survey should be absolutely final, because technologies and expectations change. But avoid making radical survey changes or the results from different surveys can't be compared for trends.

The Challenges of Implementation

Many companies have implemented impressive service strategies, but fewer have successfully carried them out or have maintained them at the desired level of service. Committees can meet and define each objective. Existing philosophies and practices can be well understood. Guidelines for implementation can be drawn up. But actually changing the way people behave is a different matter, one that calls for complete belief in the changes you're implementing, willingness to adapt as the need arises, and outstanding leadership without being authoritarian.

One company called me in to discuss an I.S. service training program as part of their move towards Total Quality. The senior manager who I met with told me frankly that she didn't believe in all this mumbo-jumbo, but the CEO wanted it done so she'd follow through with her assignment. If this is the attitude, then it's most likely not going to succeed. The attitude has to be positive and the feeling must be belief.

Don't confuse belief with religion. Another fault is that some people adopt service as a religion and let it cloud their judgment about all other processes going on around them. Belief is simply a recognition that you're doing the right thing, and that the right thing will lead to more satisfied clients. It doesn't close your eyes to other techniques. Just the opposite of that, your desire to provide superior service keeps your eyes wide open to new opportunities to improve service.

It's tempting to try to force the new ways down people's throats. What's that you say? Oh no, not me! Managers know by experience that it's much quicker to tell people what to do than to give staff a voice in policy decisions as well as the authority to act on their own. It's at the management level that most service strategy implementations break down.

Just as the clients must be influenced in their expectations of I.S., the staff must be influenced in their attitudes toward service excellence. In both cases, there's a learning process that's rooted in respect, in sharing complete information, in understanding each other's points of view.

The Living Proof

When an effective service process is in place, you can quickly pick up the friendly language and positive staff attitude. Take a look at Figure 9-2, showing alternative approaches to language and attitude.

The first example, whether you're open or closed, is much like seeing a glass as half full or half empty. There's a lot that goes on around us that pushes us toward the half-empty, "we close at . . ." viewpoint. Our society is a competitive one. Look at what we call an overtime football game? Why is it "Sudden Death" rather than "Sudden Victory"? Think in terms of cooperation and a beginning, not in terms of death and an end.

The last example is not always easy to implement. On the whole, people prefer a live response, but they'd rather have a prompt answering machine than have the phone ring ten times before it's answered. This happens too often in a small office where people

Figure 9-2. Sample of a Service Approach

UNFRIENDLY	FRIENDLY
We close at 5:00 p.m.	We are open till 5:00 p.m.
All requests for services must be approved by four levels of management	Request for services requiring less than X days will of X $s will be approved at the local level. (or require one manager's signature)
All hardware & software requests must be approved by I.S.	All hardware and software requests within these established guidelines need not be reviewed by I.S.
Telephone answering machine	Personal response within two rings

pick up each others' phones. An answering machine is preferable to endless ringing when the office is closed, and a machine that will take messages is better than a message saying you're closed and when you'll be open. Overall, direct, prompt, personal contact sets the tone for a constructive relationship and is your goal for telephone communication. However, remember that an answering process described above should be utilized only when human interaction cannot be successfully accomplished.

We Must . . .

Figure 9-3 is a series of "must's" that IPPs should adopt.

The second item on this "must" list is especially hard for many—under-promise and over-deliver. Most of us are naturally enthusiastic when we see a good problem in front of us, and it's all too easy to believe that we can do more than we can, especially regarding time frames. This "must" item is not encouraging us to lie, but to be more conservative in our estimates. If you're a typical IPP, you most often underestimate the amount of time most projects will take.

Part of that tendency to underestimate comes from a desire to please. The client wants a short time frame and it's easier to tell her what she wants to hear and make changes later on, if necessary. Af-

Figure 9-3.

WE MUST:

- Adopt a "We own the problem" attitude.
- Learn to under-promise and over-deliver.
- Watch the body signals (client and yours).
- Inform the staff about the struggles as well as the achievements.
- Reach for complaints as an avenue to view innovative businesses.
- Periodically "show off" our service area. Let our staff be measured by their behavior.
- Empower staff to solve service issues.

ter all, it's not impossible for us to meet her timetable; it's just a push. Unfortunately, we try too often to put that "push" on most of our projects, and that can only result in tension and delays.

The fifth "must," looking at complaints as an invitation to innovation, also requires an attitude shift for most of us. As stated earlier, as a group, we tend to be defensive and to take criticism too personally. That just means that we work hard and we're proud of what we do. But we also must accept that we can always improve, and complaints will usually show us where those improvements are needed.

The last "must" is one of the hardest for managers, empowering the staff to solve service issues. "When to empower" is a difficult decision. As you begin a new service program, you may believe that your staff needs additional training before such empowerment can occur. That may well be true. But you need to be able to say, "Now we'll give them more control." Perhaps you need to create a plan that will gradually, on a predetermined schedule, give more power to the staff. That schedule can be set according to dates or milestones of training or service accomplishments that need to be reached.

Measurement Tools

Your ongoing measurement plan may use personal surveys, survey or comment cards, or client interviews. Whatever you use, be sure there's a good computerized tracking procedure that allows you to measure current results against past results and to see trends as they emerge. And tell everyone in your department the results. Share your information. We'll focus on measurement tools in Chapter 15.

The Catalysts

When I go into some companies I see catchy Quality slogans plastered on the walls. Many manufacturing sites have status charts posted everywhere. But to find out what they really think of their quality of service, I have to talk to the people, from the CEO to the mail room.

Are they enthusiastic about the changes going on? Do they readily identify a couple people who are really making things happen, or who have provided exceptional service that others can emulate? Has an optimistic war broken out on bureaucracy? Do all the employees feel that they belong, that they're a part of a vital organism? Are clients uniformly treated well—and do employees consider fellow employees as clients, in addition to those outside the department or division, or organization? Do they believe that, if they have a problem, they can either fix it themselves, or that someone will listen to their concern and then act to resolve it?

There are numerous clichés telling us that the proof is in the pudding. For outstanding service, the action has to be from the heart and from the mind, not from the lips or the posters.

Here is a list of actions that must be done, I believe must be done with the heart and with the mind:

- Get involved
- Live the service philosophy
- Create heroes, in your client groups as well as IPP staff
- Open channels of communication from the front line up
- Talk it up and show it up
- Declare war on red tape
- Make everyone someone's client

PERSONAL ACTION PLAN

Worksheet

DELIVER WHAT CLIENTS REALLY WANT

Specific ideas I can use on the job:

Specific actions I will take within 30 days:

Chapter 10

Building the I.S./ Client Relationship

"Always assume your opponent to be smarter than you."
—Walther Rathenau

Four Types of I.S. Service

I.S. serves more clients than just business or internal departments. This chapter shows examples of four different client bases and how some I.S. organizations have greatly expanded their client base.

Unlike any other function within the corporation, we serve a variety of clients. Of the following four client bases, the first two are more common; and the second two are becoming common.

The first two focus on clients within your corporation.

1. Internal Service Within the Corporation

Here's our traditional, primary role, serving other departments within our corporation at both local and remote locations. Examples are I.S. serving a sales department, an accounting department, or a manufacturing or a distribution group.

127

> *If you have a seasoned I.S. department and you haven't looked outside your organization to expand your service base, and there's nothing restricting you from doing so, it may well be worth exploring.*

2. Internal Service Within I.S.

These are our colleagues within the I.S. group. It may be an operations group serving the application folks. We don't often look at those on our "team" as being clients, but they are—and we should. We can no longer exist and operate as several individual islands of support. We need to work as a cohesive team and provide quality service to each other, treating each other as the clients that we are.

3. External Service Within I.S.

These are people in I.S. groups at other companies. It's becoming more common for an I.S. department to market and deliver products and services to other companies' I.S. organizations.

4. External Service External to I.S.

I know most of you have heard much about SABRE and its successes but, I thought it would be worth repeating here from a service perspective. The SABRE Airline System was developed by American Airlines and used by travel agents worldwide. Robert Crandall, the Chairman of American Airlines, was asked an awkward question at a recent Society of Information Management (SIM) Conference. "If you were forced to sell the airline or SABRE, which would you sell?" His answer—the airline, because SABRE is so profitable.

SABRE revolutionized the industry by linking customers to central data bases. The same procedure has been used by Otis Elevator Company. OTISLINE is their service-dispatching system. It operates 24 hours a day, 365 days a year, and assign field mechanics to repair sites for routine service calls in an average time of 76 minutes.

If you have a seasoned I.S. department and you haven't looked outside your organization to expand your service base, and there's nothing restricting you from doing so, it may well be worth exploring.

Seven Steps to Long-Lasting Relationships

Lists are easy to compile. Every writer and theorist will give you the "Five Easy Steps" to something or other. The reason why you're given so many of those "Five Easy Steps" is because people buy them ("buy" as both "purchase" and "accept"), and then they try to memorize them, maybe even live by them. But what very few people do is thoroughly understand all the assumptions and premises that lie beneath that handy-dandy, easy-to-memorize, change-your-life list.

We've gone into a lot of detail so far. And I've provided my share of lists. Here's another (Figure 10-1)—and I just want to be sure that you'll think about all the reasons beneath its outer simplicity.

Contact

Step 1 is Contact. You won't get clients by theorizing about how to work with them, so get out there and meet them. This initial contact is crucial. Always put your best foot forward. As I travel, I find people don't think much about the process of making the contact, but this is your first impression. If you're not seriously thinking professionally about making the contact, it's unlikely that the professional service quality you want to provide will be there after the initial contact. The first contact sets the tone for what's to come.

Rapport

Step 2 is Rapport. If you have confidence in yourself and in your service, then you can be natural, casual yet business-like. Most people assume they're naturally good at rapport.

Let's test your idea of rapport. You come to my office. I'm a prospective client. You look around and notice the pictures of my kids on my desk, and seeing this as an ice-breaker you ask, "Are those your kids?" Is that a good start for building rapport?

My instinctive answer to your question is likely to be, "No, I borrowed them for the weekend." If the pictures are sitting on my desk, and I'm about the right age to have such kids, then the odds are 99% that they're my kids. To me, you've asked a dumb question to start off. No good.

Figure 10-1.   7 Steps to Long Lasting I.S./Client Relationships

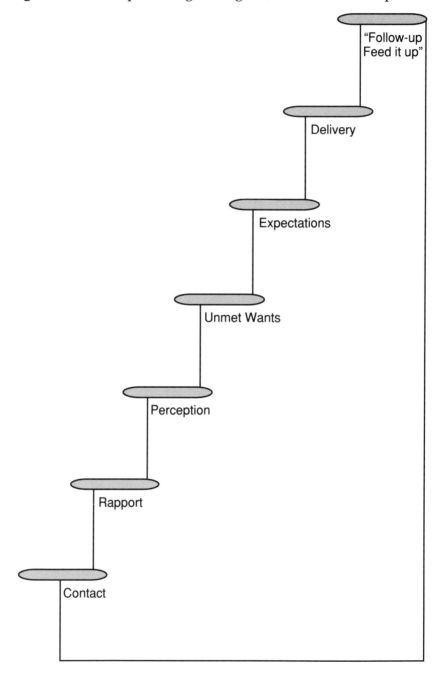

What if you phrase your opener a little differently and comment, "Those are good-looking kids." That's better. It may be overt flattery, but most people aren't offended by it. What if my response is, "Yeah, and let me tell you what happened last night. My wife asked me for a divorce, and I'm telling you, she's not gonna get those kids. I don't care what she wants or about the rules for divorce, she's not gettin' those kids. I mean, those kids are my kids, you know what I'm saying? I've spent a lotta time bringin' up those kids, just as much as she did. Just because I go out with the guys once in a while, I mean, you know how men are, I'm not gonna lose my kids. See that little girl right there? She's the apple of my eye, I mean, she . . ."

Are you building rapport? No. As a professional, when something gets this personal, drop it and get out of there as quickly as can professionally be done. He's not likely in the right frame of mind for a solid business discussion. Don't get involved. A casual comment about home or hobby is fine, but don't be a shoulder to cry on. You just don't know how the potential client will react later on. A common reaction is for the client to be embarrassed by the outburst and try to avoid the person who heard the confession.

There's nothing wrong with idle chit-chat at the start of a meeting, or while waiting for others to arrive, but here are a few rules to observe:

A. If there are only two of you, and you're asking questions or making comments that get one word responses, drop it. This is not a chit-chat kind of guy.

B. If there are only two of you, and you get the beginning of a confessional, as above, drop it, but do it tactfully so as not to offend.

C. If you're in a group, be sensitive to who's there. I've seen situations where the beginning talk was always sports, and someone who doesn't care about sports felt excluded. A joke with sexual innuendo is not only in bad taste, it may result in a harassment case against the teller. Be sensitive to the composition of the entire group, and don't exclude.

Your goal in rapport-building is simply to have a situation where you and the person or people you're with are comfortable with each other. Read the signs you receive from other people, and those signs will be non-verbal more often than verbal, and then react accordingly.

Perception

Step 3 is Perception, but Step 3 began before Step 1. You've worked to establish the perceptions of present and prospective clients. Now that you're in contact, you must naturally project the image of cooperation and concern that you've been working to project. You need to do your best to help determine how others perceive you, then be sensitive to clues for how they really do think of you. What they perceive is reality to them. How they think they need to work with us may be totally out of sync with what we really do.

Unmet Wants

Step 4 is Unmet Wants. Throughout your preliminary work with the client, you must be reading between the lines. Perhaps there will be needs she has but that she's not mentioning because she doesn't think you can help. Or perhaps her mental processes make jumps that yours don't make. When a process is second nature to someone, she's likely to leave out steps in the description because they seem so obvious that they don't need mentioning. But you don't know the process that well. You need to hear them. You must "hear between the words" (the verbal equivalent of "read between the lines"). You must ask the right questions to be sure you get to these unmet wants.

Expectations

Step 5 is Expectations. Lay it out. And what we lay out should be expectations that we can meet or exceed. Here's what we can do. Here's how long it will take. Here's what it will cost. Here's how we'll do it. These are the expected deliverables. If we extend ourselves in our deliverables so that we'll have a tough time just meeting them, then we're causing our own troubles.

Delivery

Step 6 is Delivery. You stated the deliverables. Now deliver them. Deliver the end product that the client expects, in the manner and form that the client expects it. No last minute surprises.

Follow-up/Feed It Up

Step 7 is "Follow-up/Feed it up." Evaluate how the relationship has gone and is still going. Check in periodically. And publicize successes. Make sure people hear about things we've done well.

Just as there are four types of I.S. service, we have defined four distinct styles of delivering that service.

Service Styles

We divide the IPPs working with clients into four different styles of service. They are:

> Untapped Resource
> Provider
> Counselor
> Problem-solver

Let's define each style before we examine how each is needed. Figure 10-2 analyses each style from three perspectives: The role the IPP sees herself in, the primary focus she has while providing service, and the tasks that are most important to her.

Following is a brief description of each style: This definition is to convey the styles and roles they perform noting that not one style is totally right or totally wrong. Please evaluate them against your current organization. In achieving client service ask yourself, "Is the style or mix of styles appropriate?

The Untapped Resource

This person's role is to be a survivor. The person rarely volunteers for anything, does his job acceptably, and is usually there to help out or fill in the cracks in jobs that have to be done. His focus is on preserving his own self-interest. The tasks seen as most important on a regular basis are centered around making life on the job as painless as possible.

Figure 10-2. Styles of Serving the I.S. Client

Style	Untapped Resource	Provider	Counselor	Problem-Solver
Role	SURVIVOR	VENDOR	LISTENER	CONSULTANT
Focus	Preserving self interest	Delivering technical products and services as specified by the client	Understanding the individual point of view of the client	Contributing to the long range goals of the business through information management
Task	☐ Making it through the day ☐ Making it easier for themselves ☐ Controlling stress ☐ Educating the client	☐ Reacting to requests ☐ Taking orders ☐ Meeting client specifications ☐ Taking quick action, delivery and response	☐ Giving individual attention and help ☐ Understanding the unique situation of the client ☐ Determining problem areas ☐ Calming upset clients	☐ Knowing the business of the business ☐ Accessing top management ☐ Satisfying unmet wants ☐ Educating the client

When this description is written down, it sounds like someone who's just not a contributor, but that's wrong. Because the person is a survivor, he knows how to fill in when needed, knows how to follow instructions, knows how to do a good job. It's just that the motivation for doing well is external, not internal. When the workload is heavy, this untapped resource can become extremely valuable by doing whatever is necessary to keep the operation moving forward. What percentage of the IPPs in your organization fit this category?

The Provider

The provider takes the role of a vendor. A vendor is someone who sells a product. In this case, the product is I.S. services. Back in Chapter 3 we discussed levels of service. They are economy, satisfaction, and care. Take at look back at Figure 3-2 on page 32 and then say where you think the provider fits in. Most likely it's at the satisfaction level.

A provider will work hard to deliver just what the client requests. The work will be done with both care and quality, but simply providing won't go so far as to turn the customer into a long-term client. Objectives are more based on speed and accuracy than client relationships or exceeding expectations.

The Counselor

Everyone likes to talk with the counselor. He listens. He understands you. You're not just a face in the crowd, not just one of his many clients. The attention is focused on you. If you're upset he can help calm you down. He can get you to talk so as to find out exactly what your project problem areas are.

Can you see anything missing? The focus of the style is to listen well and pinpoint the problem, but the focus is more on problem definition than speed or accuracy.

The Problem-Solver

Here's the person with the good answers, the solutions to the problem. She knows the business through and through. She'll analyze the client's problem, coming up with just the right procedure for a solution. Potential problem here is in problem definition. She may be so eager to get to the solution that she doesn't spend enough time evaluating the total problem.

Blending the Styles

Figure 10-3, "Plotting the Service Styles," shows a graph of the service styles. See if you can assign a percentage of the time your I.S. organization spends in each of the four sections. Is the percentage heaviest in one or two sections? What does that say about us? Are we good providers but low on counseling? Are we high in problem-solving but low in untapped resources?

Figure 10-3.   Plotting the Service Styles

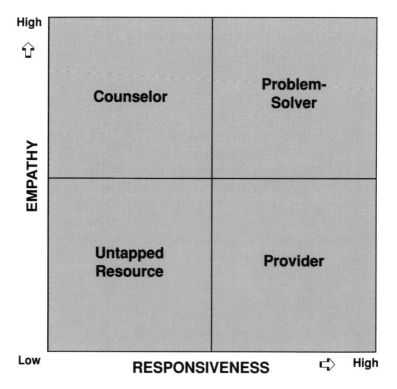

Let's turn to the individual approach to service styles—your approach. Think of various interactions you've had over the past 24 hours with everyone who qualifies as a business client. Remember to include colleagues in your department. First, on a separate sheet, list the interactions. Don't take a half-hour meeting as one occurrence; divide each interaction into how your organization approaches interactions.

Then, next to each interaction, list the one (or perhaps two, maybe even three) service styles you followed. Once that's completed, plot them. If the interaction showed you as 100% Counselor, then place an "X" right in the middle of the Counselor square. If you were an equal blend of Provider and Problem-Solver, then the X goes on the line between them, at the far right.

Figure 10-4 is an example of part of one day, and how it would be plotted. Before you do your own graph, you may want to make copies of this page so that you can use this exercise again.

Figure 10-4. Sample Style Analysis

Meeting with Janet Johnson of Sales regarding revised database

General greeting	Provider/Problem-Solver
JJ explains problem	Counselor/Problem-Solver
I probe with questions	Problem-Solver
I describe alternative approaches	Problem-Solver
She comments and I respond	Problem-Solver/Counselor
I explain how I'll prepare proposal	Problem-Solver/Provider
We discuss time frames	Provider

I return to my office

Determine how to spend next 1/2 hour	Untapped Resource
Make follow-up calls to clients	Counselor/Untapped Res.

When applied to the graph, this Style Analysis yields an example that then could be plotted on Figure 10-5.

Figure 10-5.   Style Analysis Plotted

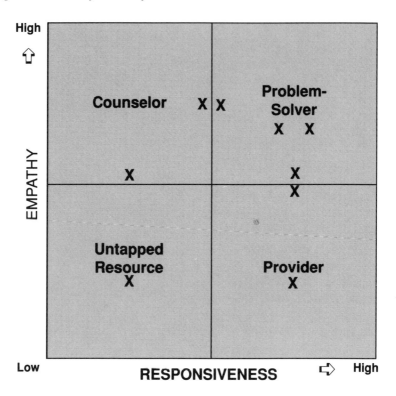

As Figure 10-5 shows, the time being analyzed has some balance to it, but with an emphasis on the Problem-Solver style.

In the Sample Style Analysis, it's not necessarily the activity that
determines how an interaction gets categorized; it's the attitude while
carrying it out. I can probe with questions as a Counselor, a Problem-Solver, or a Provider. It depends on a blend of my motivation
for asking questions, my sensitivity to the responses, and how I process those responses.

This is a useful exercise because it forces you to analyze your
own service performance in a way by focusing on why you do what
you do, and how you respond to people and to information. It's also
more comfortable to take a test when there are no right or wrong
answers. An I.S. department needs all kinds of service styles in dif-

ferent blends. Different clients respond best to different styles. Frank may need someone who's high on the empathy, someone with a strong Counselor quality, while Abby may prefer working with a no-nonsense, let's-get-the-work-done person, who'll be a blend of Problem-Solver and Provider.

This goes back to your Client Profile. You need to understand your client organization and your individual clients if you're going to do your best to respond to their needs.

A Departmental Analysis

Now analyze your department as a whole, or your particular group within your department. You're not just looking at individuals; you're looking at how the group is perceived by the clients. Take the four categories, Counselor, Problem-Solver, Untapped Resource, and Provider, and assign percentages to each style so that they accurately reflect your work group and add up to 100%. How appropriate is the blend? What do you want the balance to be?

You can ask clients to evaluate you in the same way, as we've done with earlier evaluations. Then compare their perceptions with what you expected their perceptions to be.

PERSONAL ACTION PLAN

Worksheet

BUILDING THE I.S./CLIENT RELATIONSHIP

Specific ideas I can use on the job:

Specific actions I will take within 30 days:

Chapter 11

Managing Expectations

"Never promise more than you can perform."

—*Publilius Syrus*

Respect and Understanding

Almost from the start of this book, managing the client expectations has been stated as one of the keys to success. Now it's time to give you some practical techniques for setting and maintaining those expectations.

But first, what do you want your clients' expectations to be? Most likely, you want them to have respect for you and to anticipate a positive solution to their problem. I believe both of those expectations are necessary if you're to be the computer service provider of first choice. You also want their expectations to be realistic. This is very important because otherwise they might expect the moon on a silver platter. This problem can occur if they really don't understand what you do. You want them to think of you as providing very high quality service, but not so high that you can't impress them by exceeding their expectations. This can work only if you work towards expectations that are idealistic rather than realistic.

Computer Magic

Mark Fox, a Professor at the University of Toronto and a recognized authority on applying emerging computer technologies to practical manufacturing problems, has said that you must always promise less than you can deliver. Then you must consistently reinforce that expectation. Your client's expectations seem to take seed from the winds of change and you must keep tamping down the soil. When you're giving people something new, and it's on a computer, many people unconsciously equate that with magic, have little sense of technological limitations, and will always want more than you deliver.

Determining Quality Service

We earlier defined Service Quality as the whole formed by all those tiny Moments of Truth. How do you measure that Quality? Different ways to take measurements have been discussed, but often knowing what to measure is part of the problem. Here's a formula for measuring quality.

Results measured against Expectations balanced with tolerance equal perceived Service Level formula R–E(T)=SL. When looking at the importance of quality service, you should look primarily at the service level that the client perceives, not your own evaluation of what is the ultimate service level that you can hypothetically deliver. What counts is not the quality of the service so much as the quality of the service that the client perceives. And perceived quality is the difference between what the client expects and what the client gets.

As an example, think of the last time that you went to Human Resources for service. It doesn't matter whether it was for information about the pension plan, inquiring about job openings for a friend, or questioning the way your HMO handled a transaction. What were your expectations? Were you pleased with the results?

I intentionally chose Human Resources for this example because opinions often vary more widely about HR than about other departments. Some may consider HR the glue that holds the organization together, while others may wonder why they need so many people as overhead and its effect on the bottom line. When someone's job is so different from your own that you don't really understand what they do, it's easy to disparage them. Note the similarity here to people who see us as creating magic?

Now go back to your HR example. What if you went in with a different attitude, having either more or less respect for them than you do? What if you had few expectations because of a lack of dealing with them in the past? Smooth, competent handling of your problem can be viewed as magnificent service if your expectations are low. If you look upon HR as always going that extra mile for the employees, then "smooth, competent" service may be a disappointment.

You must maintain high personal and departmental standards for service quality, but you're going to wind up being judged by perceived service quality.

Managing, Meeting, and Exceeding Expectations

Here are sixteen techniques to help you address your clients' expectations. Many of these ideas have already been brought up, but here they're placed in a precise framework for action.

1. Know Your Client

Know what your client expects. And then go the extra mile to give the client more. You want to be the service provider of choice. Your competition will likely provide good service. Yours must be better.

Develop a client profile for the key individuals within the client organizations. Learn what's important to them. What's most important for you to know to be able to influence their expectations? Stand in their shoes. What makes them tick? How can you turn them on with your service? There's no substitute for knowing your client.

2. Examine Your Business Through Your Client's Eyes

What impression do you make on someone else? Walk through your operation. Evaluate all communications that clients may receive: business cards, stationary, brochures, proposals. Are they neat, clean and professional? Is correspondence error-free? What's the procedure when a client calls into the department? If you're not sure of the exact way someone is treated on the phone, have someone call in for you and find out. When you're talking on the phone, imagine you're your customer and see if you're pleased with how you're being treated. As you've done before, analyze each MOT your client experiences.

3. Turn the Expectations on Yourself

What level of service would you expect? What's most important? What's less important? Your own emotional hot buttons may be similar to your client's. But don't assume that they're the same. While it's valuable to determine what you would want as a client, it's also valuable to practice what I call The Ungolden Rule. As stated by playwright George Bernard Shaw, "It is unwise to do unto others as you would have them do unto you. Their tastes may not be the same."

4. Make Clients Feel Safe, Secure, and Valued

Clients decide emotionally and justify with logic. Clients need to feel respected. They need to feel like they are part of the contribution, not just the recipient of your services. From the moment they are greeted they need to feel that you are glad to see them. That their needs will at least be seriously considered, if not resolved. Give the client the facts in a way the client can best use the information.

5. Influence Expectations

If your client doesn't come to you with clear expectations, adopt your best counseling style, then influence and define those expectations by working together as a team to set them.

Nothing helps set expectations more than consistency. If you treat a client the same way each time, the client will soon expect that treatment. Establish and build rapport on every encounter.

- Smile sincerely
- Keep a relaxed and open posture
- Make the client feel at ease and accepted
- Ask open questions
- Keep track of personal interests
- Learn about the client's professional background

> **Sometimes clients need the first example of your service before they set their expectations.**

As another example of setting expectations, many clients will only see their immediate need and not understand that there's a larger systems problem indicated by that single need. You can show them that your job is to understand and address both the immediate and the long-range solutions. In a similar vein, show that your understanding is not just for the client's specific need, but that you understand how that need fits into the larger scope of the organization. These two instances show the breadth of your work.

6. Set the Tone From the Start

Sometimes clients need the first example of your service before they set their expectations. If you'd spent the last ten years only going to fast food restaurants (because of the kids' preferences, of course) and then finally go to a classy, four star restaurant, you're not going to know what to expect for service until you see it. If your client hasn't used your services before, work with them to set the expectations. Offer a hypothetical procedure, a prototype, for how you'll provide service and then ask, "How well does this meet your needs?," and "How can we improve it?"

From the start, show respect for the client's time, intellect and pressures. This kind of respect encourages a mutual respect from them. If you're being realistic and fair with them, they're more likely to be the same with you.

7. Tell Clients What To Expect

Let them know what they can expect from working with you. Nothing sets immediate expectations better than simply telling them what you'll do. Present a plan of action that is flexible and accommodates the client's needs.

8. Tell Clients Your Expectations

Educate your clients on what they have to do to get maximum benefit from your services. Let them know that you also have expectations of how they'll help you work efficiently. This acknowledgment of a two-way street, if done well, sets a tone of realism and cooperation.

9. Customize Your High Standards

Tailor your high standards to the service each client desires. Client expectations differ. Deliver customized service whenever possible.

10. Know Your Clients Needs Better Than They Do

This begins with knowing your client. Seek to understand before being understood. Let the client do 80% of the talking, and when the client is talking, listen, listen, and listen harder. Then ask plenty of questions. In advance, plan five to ten questions that when answered will tell you exactly what they need. Then later verify your views by comparing with others or by supporting with documentation and data. A detailed understanding of their needs demonstrates the depth of your solutions.

11. Deliver More Than You Promise

Underpromise—but not flagrantly. Lower your risk of failure. Here are a couple examples.

- If you expect you may be able to deliver an answer to a client on Monday, tell him he'll have it Tuesday.
- If you must give a cost estimate, go on the high end of the possible range.
- If she needs five new features added to an application and you think you probably can do it, but know it'll be a push, promise four.
- If you believe the job should take four months if all goes smoothly, estimate five months, or six.

This is not lying, so don't be uncomfortable. Most IPPs work hard to deliver the best service and quality of work that they can, but they also tend to overestimate the results, or their skills, or the time frame.

By underpromising, you're likely being more realistic than if you gave your initial estimate. You're only balancing your natural optimism with a strong dose of reality.

To phrase this in a totally positive way, deliver more than you promise.

12. Keep In Touch

Let them know you are thinking about them. Absence can break down confidence in your work and it keeps you from reinforcing the expectations that you've set. By staying in touch you'll be aware of changing needs or situations. You can continue to educate your client about your services and products. And there are many ways to keep in touch, besides the telephone and the memo. Newsletters, department announcements, open houses, demonstrations of products are all possible. Send articles that discuss related problems. Take advantage of chance encounters; don't just pass by with a "hi." Build the relationship.

13. Keep Your Clients Informed

As an addition to "keep in touch," keep your clients informed of what's going on in your organization. An understanding of the complexity and variety of services I.S. provides will help them appreciate what you are doing for them.

14. Use Problems To Show Your Service Quality

Providing the right solutions, and being sure your client is aware of alternatives and reasons for your decisions will help them respect your work.

15. Encourage Complaints

Pay attention to them when you get them. Use them to identify ways of improving and changing client demands.

16. Help Clients Understand the Deliverables

Give your clients what they need and help them understand that they have received what they needed. Use third-party testimony.

Controlling Through Service

By following these sixteen techniques you're controlling through service. If you provide valuable services to your clients, chances are they are going to include I.S. in the strategies and real management of their business. The result is a much better understanding of the businesses you serve. This increased understanding helps you exceed their expectations.

PERSONAL ACTION PLAN

Worksheet

MANAGING EXPECTATIONS

Specific ideas I can use on the job:

Specific actions I will take within 30 days:

Chapter 12

Creating Satisfied Clients

"Keep your cool and you command everybody."
                                        —*Louis de Saint-Just*

Client Satisfaction

Don't be content if you're effectively managing and meeting client expectations. Strive to exceed them.

Let's look back at a few of the concepts we've discussed. What does "client satisfaction" really mean. Put a check in the right box.

- You have reached your high performance service goals.
- You have done enough to keep the client happy.
- You have given the client better service quality than what was expected.

The first choice was tempting, but it's not correct. Yes, you want to reach your high performance goals, but your goals are set according to your understanding of your clients. If you reach your goals, then you're only certain of satisfying yourself. Your ultimate goal, "client satisfaction," must refer to your client. As we've seen, perceived Service Level is Results measured against Expectations balance with

151

> **Don't be content if you're effectively managing and meeting client expectations. Strive to exceed them.**

some client tolerance. When you've given your client better service than expected, then you've reached client satisfaction.

The Service Provider

That was just a refresher to keep us all on course. This section will focus on you—on the service provider. There are a number of characteristics that we feel the service providers must have to achieve client satisfaction.

Service providers must:

- Believe in the system
- Believe in themselves
- Have high self-esteem
- Take responsibility and ownership of the job
- Feel a part of the team
- See themselves contributing to something important
- Take on heroic emotional labor

Belief in the Process

I've said that a common place where good service plans fall apart is at the point of weak follow through. Many of us find that the new behaviors we must learn feel foreign. We find it hard to accept that giving up immediate, total control will result in a system that has a stronger common direction and purpose.

This resembles the new science of chaos, where the end result of the system is predictable, but the specific actions of the individual parts are not. My New Hampshire business colleague Dick Morley, inventor of the programmable controller and CEO of Flavors Technology, a manufacturing supercomputer company, has a good parallel for this phenomenon—a flock of birds.

We often admire their teamwork as they fly overhead. If we were to capture their activity on a computer, the model we'd create would likely be quite complex. By traditional means we'd create a lead bird to monitor the flight of the flock. The bigger the flock, the smarter this central brain must be and the better communications between birds must be. This is how most of us have managed, and we've often seen communications breakdown as the flock grows bigger.

But Mother Nature doesn't work that way. Each bird gets the same information from shared resources, in this case the environment. Then the rules are simple. Fly three feet from the bird on each side, fly at a steady speed, slow down when turning, and head for the roost. Note that there's no central processor or manager guiding all these birds.

In the old days, we called this delegation. Today we call it empowerment. The difference is in the employee's authority to make more decisions on his own. In I.S., if all staff members know how to react, know their responsibilities, and are sensitive to clients, then we can't predict at any one time where a particular staff member will be or what she'll be doing, but we can still predict the outcome—client satisfaction. The entire staff is working from a common philosophy, and each knows how to take charge or cooperate with team members in whatever the situation must be, and each has the authority for significant action.

As empowerment began to move into factories, there was an obstacle that management didn't always anticipate: worker distrust. This is still often the case when empowerment begins, whether in factories or in white collar areas like I.S. If the old management style is authoritarian, and it's been that way for as long as Hal can remember (and he's been here for 38 years), then why should Hal think that things will change just because management says they will. "If we've been treated like sheep before, then we'll be treated like sheep again, and this teamwork and service quality stuff will just be a blip on the continuum of management authority." Well, maybe Hal doesn't talk like that, but the sentiment is all too common.

Self-Esteem

To accept the new management style, at all levels of management, the people who report to that manager must have sufficient self-esteem. They must respect their own abilities, the importance of the work they do, and feel that they're a part of a larger whole. Most often, that's a comradeship with a small team of employees you interact with daily.

If that esteem doesn't exist in a majority of the employees, then increasing self-esteem should be worked at before announcing any major, overall change in the manner of doing business. When top management announces a huge change in service quality, but employees can't yet see any evidence of change in the works, then skepticism will be everywhere.

Preparing the Employees

A friend in a high management position in a major division of one of our country's largest corporations (to remain nameless for obvious reasons) told me how all the employees of this division were brought together in a huge hall. Managers, custodians, sales, and secretaries were all grouped together. The company clearly wanted to give the impression of equality and "we're all in this together." Top officers of the corporation then gave an high-power, inspiring presentation about the move to Total Quality. Three weeks after the meeting, no one had seen any evidence of change, and employees at all levels were making fun of the big meeting.

The corporation had the right intentions, but there was nothing in progress, no changes impending, to give the staff any sign of sincerity. Activity was undoubtedly going on behind the scenes, but by the time the results of that planning reach the workers, the whole Total Quality move will be viewed as a farce.

The best of motives doesn't help unless there's visible evidence of change that corresponds to the message being delivered.

Rules for Service Success

Let's assume that management at all levels and the entire staff is working together for service quality. Here are five simple rules for

IPPs to follow that, from a behavioral perspective, should ensure service success.

1. Be concerned with clients first.
2. Be earnest and sincere.
3. Be confident and enthusiastic.
4. Be natural and unassuming.
5. Be consistent in your service quality.

These rules complement each other. For example, if you're unassuming, then you're likely to be concerned with the customer first. Yet that first rule is likely to be the hardest to follow for many of us. It means we don't put the technology first, we don't allow our ideas for solutions and enthusiasm for new technology to dominate over our concern for the needs of the clients. We must listen, listen, listen.

Interpersonal Skills

Those five rules all assume that you have strong and natural interpersonal skills. Not everyone does. Thomas Watson, founder of IBM, said, "If you don't genuinely like your clients, the chances are they won't buy." Few would disagree. What happens in a move to superior service if you genuinely prefer a computer to a client?

This is a situation that is often mishandled. In some situations, if an organization is revising its approach to its market, people who don't exhibit the primary skills needed will be let go. Often new people who've exhibited such skills will be hired. This can only create dissension as people wonder, "Will I be the next to go?"

Such dissension is not necessary. What's necessary is an analysis of a person's dominant skills and interests, and then fitting that person into a job that will leverage those skills. For example, if Nancy naturally stays up on the newest technologies and loves exploring whether they're appropriate for in-house applications, but does not do well at building professional relationships, then the company should use her skills to its advantage. If I.S. is serving a client as a team, not everyone on your team will be a primary contact for the customer. Nancy can be a voice contributing suggestions and evaluations relating to new techniques, can contribute to development of the application, and can spend most of her time at the computer, not with customers.

As a service quality emphasis is developed, there are bound to be some shifting jobs. However, if handled well, people will see that the shifts are into positions that take advantage of their dominant skills and interests, and the disruption that naturally accompanies job changes will be minimized.

Offer Rewards

If you provide information leading to the arrest and conviction of Jesse James, train robber, you will receive a reward of $10,000!

When the term "reward" is mentioned, that's often the first type of reward people think of. Or perhaps this. When your puppy is learning to use the great outdoors rather than your oriental carpet, what do you give him each time he's successful in this new endeavor? When your child doesn't want to _____ (fill in the blank—go to dancing school? Visit Uncle Bernard? Eat vegetables?), what do you often do, even though books about how to be a good parent tell you not to? You give a reward. You might even call it a bribe.

Why do you give these rewards? Because it's human nature to do what gets rewarded. Let's raise the level of discussion so that we're considering rewards for outstanding client service—perhaps a reward to you. Are you insulted because you were only doing your job? That's not likely. It's much more likely that you're pleased that your management has recognized how hard you're working and what a good job you've done.

Each I.S. department should create a system that rewards superior client service. This was mentioned as Objective #10 in Chapter 9. Rewards don't need to be money, in fact they rarely are. Often the most meaningful reward is having the boss come up to you individually, shake your hand, and sincerely thank you for your superior work on a specific project. Each department has to determine what kinds of rewards are best for them. Recognition dinners held annually or bi-annually are popular, where individuals and/or teams receive plaques recognizing outstanding service. Sometimes the reward may be a gift certificate to a restaurant or store. If the reward goes to a team, the reward may be something that maintains the team's comradery, such as group tickets to a game or concert.

The particular reward system your I.S. department implements is not what's important. It's the fact that one is implemented.

Build Strong Links

Things won't always go as planned. There will be rough spots in your relations with your clients, no matter how well you plan and how effectively you work. How will you survive those unsteady times? Will you have built up enough credit in your client's emotional bank account so that you can make a withdrawal without making the balance disastrously low?

Let me explain. As the service provider, we're in the situation where we give much more than we take. It's the nature of our job. People have come to us looking for assistance. Each time we respond and help in a way that's beyond what they expected, we're creating greater credibility in their eyes. They trust us more each time we exceed expectations, and that can be as small as returning a phone call promptly, sending a manual you think they may need even before they request it, or making the phone call to see how they're doing.

On the other hand, each time we disappoint a client, we come down a notch in their sight. And it can be the same apparently minor types of occurrences that are sending us down: a phone call doesn't get returned, a requested manual doesn't promptly get sent, installing the deliverables and then forgetting about them.

Each time you exceed expectations, you're making a deposit in your emotional bank account. When times are tough, a few withdrawals may be necessary, but you should take care to maintain a positive balance.

The Emotional Bank Account

You need a bank book for your records. Figure 12-1 shows a way to record all your transactions.

As another exercise, you might get together with several of your colleagues who work with you in providing service to a particular client and review the activities of the past few months in the light of an emotional bank account. Are you maintaining a positive balance?

Figure 12-1.   Emotional Bank Account

NAME: _____

DEPOSITS MADE		WITHDRAWALS	
Date	Description	Date	Description

Basic Problem-Solving Questions

There are a number of simple techniques to help you solve client problems. Let's see how basic we can get. To solve a problem, ask these questions:

- What is the task being discussed?
- What is the current manual or computer-based solution?
- What is right and what is wrong with this solution?
- What problems are being caused by this solution?
- What would you like the solution to be?
- What would you like the situation to be?

Seeing the Big Picture

Those two final questions only vary in substituting the word "situation" for "solution." By "solution," I mean the technical output of the application. By "situation," I mean the business result that the solution contributes to.

This distinction is part of your work to help the client see the whole problem. The client may believe that a new or revised computerized solution will solve the problem when a major contributor to the problem may be how the current computerized solution is being applied.

"It's a computer error," isn't only a cop out. It's often demonstrating ignorance of the real problem. As the service provider of choice, you must understand a broader perspective. You must understand how your computer application will fit into the big picture. You must take a systems perspective of the situation.

Even though your specialization is I.S. and you can't be expected to understand all the ramifications of a client's business, you can raise the appropriate questions so that the client won't be looking to the computer to solve problems that are more human than technical.

Seeking Long-Term Satisfaction

If your client wants, or only sees, the immediate pressing need, your job is to solve that need as quickly as possible *AND* to understand the long-range ramifications. If the expressed need only is a stop-gap measure and doesn't address the real problem, you should be sure the real, longer-range problem gets discussed. You and your client are working together for long-range satisfaction.

Here are some guidelines for achieving long-term client satisfaction.

- Show concern and empathy. Worry for the success of the client.
- If you or I.S. is at fault, take the blame in a straightforward manner. Apologize sincerely.
- Look for problems you can solve.
- Try to create immediate satisfaction by taking action quickly on anything you can.
- Never tell the client your problems. Most don't care and the rest are happy to see someone else worse off than they are.
- Be positive, *stay calm*, and use a problem-solving approach.

You noticed my emphasis on staying calm? Always show your client that you're in control. In reality your stomach may be churning away, but stay calm. Remain the thorough professional.

"Look for problems you can solve." It sounds logical, but if it were so easy it wouldn't be a point that we repeat in various forms throughout this book. When determining your deliverables, take into account your current technical abilities, your manpower availability, and the current department workload. Examine the skills needed by the client to implement the new solution. How much training will they need? Once you've announced what you can do for your client, you can't backtrack without draining your emotional bank account, or bombing most of your bridges.

"Taking action quickly" deserves special mention. Nothing builds confidence in your work like a little success. Sometimes it won't take long to make a noticeable change in the client's situation, but it will takes months to get to the root of the problem and apply a solution. Incremental solutions, or incremental installation of a full solution, will allow the clients to see progress and share in the benefits of your progressing solution before it's complete.

Common Client Desires

The client comes to you and wants *economy*. You show the client that economy does not mean getting something cheap, it means getting outstanding value for the money.

The client seeks *safety*. You provide the references, testimonials, examples, guarantees, and atmosphere to provide that feeling of safety.

The client demands *quality*. You set the client's expectations so that they are realistic and provide you with not only the prospect of success, but with a good shot at exceeding expectations.

A Client "Bill of Rights"

You can meet those most common client desires. Let's expand those three desires into a list of ten expectations. We've created the client "Bill of Rights," indicating what every client has the right to expect from us.

Let's briefly discuss each item in the list.

1. Expect you to acknowledge his or her presence. This can be done by making eye contact if you are in a person-to-person mode or by answering the phone within two rings when a client calls.

2. Expect the undivided attention and courtesy of a professional. Don't accept any phone calls or other distractions while you are helping a client. What type of message does it send to your client if you are constantly excusing yourself to answer the phone or talk with another person?

3. Expect to be recognized as knowledgeable. Never assume your client isn't knowledgeable. Many times they may know more about the technology than you do, but may not be able to get a new software package up and running. Help educate your clients by working with them to provide a solution. Make sure you find out the facts before you assess the situation.

4. Expect you to listen to him or her. Sincerely listen to your clients, especially if they are disgruntled or upset. Find out what services the client might need. Try to understand the situation from your client's perspective.

Figure 12-2. A Client "Bill of Rights"

A Client has the right to:

1. Expect you to acknowledge his or her presence.
2. Expect the undivided attention and courtesy of a professional.
3. Expect to be recognized as knowledgeable.
4. Expect you to listen to him or her.
5. Expect you to provide prompt and accurate service.
6. Expect you to deliver what you say you will.
7. Expect a progress report or an update of the situation.
8. Expect you to accept complaints and criticism gracefully and openly in a caring manner.
9. Expect an explanation when something goes wrong.
10. Expect a "no-hassle" satisfaction guarantee.

5. Expect you to provide prompt and accurate service. Provide reliable on-time service to your clients with a courtesy-first attitude. Keep a "we need the client, and the client does not need us" attitude. Think of your clients as number one.

6. Expect you to deliver what you say you will. Be honest, up-front and sincere. Never promise things you can't deliver. Breaking promises is no way to earn respect as a superior service provider.

7. Expect a progress report or an update of the situation. Return phone calls in a reasonable amount of time. Don't make clients keep calling you for updates. Take the proactive, not reactive, mindset. Make clients know that their concerns are your most important concerns.

8. Expect you to accept complaints and criticism gracefully and openly in a caring manner. Listen actively to what the client is saying. Don't interrupt. Encourage the client to vent frustrations. Empathize with your client to show you understand why she is upset. Never lose your cool. Ask your client to suggest a way to resolve the problem. Finally, always finish on a positive note.

9. Expect an explanation when something goes wrong. Don't let your client be surprised. Contact him or her and explain what has happened and how you are going to rectify the problem. This demonstrates that you are truly concerned about your clients. You may be pleased to learn how really understanding your clients are if you involve them in this process.

10. Expect a "no-hassle" satisfaction guarantee. Make necessary retribution or correct the problem. Make clients want to do business with you in the future.

PERSONAL ACTION PLAN

Worksheet

CREATING SATISFIED CLIENTS

Specific ideas I can use on the job:

Specific actions I will take within 30 days:

Chapter 13

Managing Moments of Truth

"I'm able to perceive what the issues are before they become issues."
—Stewart Alsop III

Are You Ready?

You may be meeting a prospective or existing client. Have you prepared as much as you can? Has your group brainstormed Moments of Truth that occur at such meetings? Have you taken care that all anticipated MOTs are planned for? But what about the client who comes in unannounced? After all, you do have an open door policy. Are you prepared for the drop-in? Is that a different situation?

First, if your client is expected, do your homework. Learn about the client and the business. If you were going to a job interview you wouldn't just walk into the company without knowing anything about it. If you were going to freelance a technical article you'd review several journals to see which is most appropriate for your topic and approach. And if you're having your first meeting with a client you'll learn about that client's business and recent experiences before the meeting. Don't go in cold.

Be sure handouts that clearly, attractively show what I.S. can do are stocked and convenient. If it's an ongoing client, have whatever

> **A client stopping by is an opportunity, never an interruption.**

documents are needed for the meeting ready in plenty of time so that you can review them first.

Know not only all the technical capabilities of I.S., but also all the technical training capabilities. Be prepared to discuss how you provide full solutions to problems, not just applications but also training and follow-up.

Check your mood. Do you feel like being helpful? If your client drops in unannounced, will you respond appropriately? Your response and the appropriateness of your surroundings are among the most likely MOTs to break down in an unannounced visit.

Remember, a client stopping by is an opportunity, never an interruption. (That sounds so slogan-ish when I write it, but it shouldn't be. When the client walks in, you shouldn't have to think, "Remember, this is an opportunity." Your reaction should be automatic, unthinking, and courteous because you know as a part of your being that this is an opportunity.)

Take at look at yourself and your surroundings. Is everything the client will see as you want it to be? You don't want things so messy that it'll appear that you're disorganized or overburdened. You don't want things so pristine that it'll look like you have nothing to do. Are yesterday's coffee cups thrown out or washed. Is there always a clean cup so you can offer coffee or tea, if it's appropriate?

Know what types of solutions you have to offer or give to the client. Know why you're important to them. Be confident in your abilities. Be proud of representing your I.S. department.

The Meeting

If you have a scheduled meeting, here are a few guidelines:

- Be there early.
- Describe the agenda and allow for client input.
- Establish rapport; build upon past rapport.
- Follow the lead of the client.

- Have an inquiring mind. Look, read, ask.
- Ask—Listen—Summarize—Respond.

"Follow the lead of the client" does not mean allowing the client to be in control of the meeting. It means that you shouldn't ignore comments the client makes. It's all part of listening and responding, of hearing between the words.

When the client comes to you, whether expected or unexpected, here are guidelines:

- Smile (honestly, sincerely).
- A client in the flesh is worth two on the phone.
- Give your client full attention with eye contact and body language.
- Ask—Listen—Summarize—Respond.
- Test for success.

When the meeting is held in your office, it's all too easy to be distracted by what you were doing, or visitors, or the telephone. Don't be. The phrasing ". . . with eye contact and body language" is important. If you're not fully giving the client your attention, your eyes or your body will give it away. If you think you may have an agreement to move forward on the assignment, project it hypothetically to the client. Ask, "So if we put together a proposal that can fill these needs by September, do you think it'll be a go?" Or some similar question that seeks a non-binding commitment. In our eagerness to please we, as a profession, tend to move too quickly toward a commitment.

Identifying Workable Needs

Identify those needs you can address. Unless your client knows both computers and your business well, it's unlikely that he will have your work scoped out for you. You need to be consistent in how you work to determine addressable needs.

No no's. Drop the word "no" from your vocabulary when discussing a potential project. If it's something you can't do, then explore why the client feels it needs to be done. Either see if it can be approached differently, or if you can recommend someone else to help.

The point is, don't shut the client's concern, complaint, or request off with a blunt "no." You need to keep the client talking, explaining his needs.

If you can't provide the support needed, who can? If there's not a project here for you, or if there are areas of the needs that aren't for I.S., then who can solve them? Provide names, numbers and addresses if you can.

What is the client's goal? Not the specific limited one that you'll likely be addressing, but the longer-range one that you'll be contributing to. As said before, your job is to understand how this project fits into the client's overall business and into the company's goals as well.

Let the client know when you're giving special service. This can be tricky, because, if it sounds like an act, it's easy to be perceived as the sleazy "Have I got a deal for you," type of salesperson. If you're going beyond your usual range of service in some respect, state it as a matter of fact. Don't make a big deal of it, but say it so that the client knows it.

Figure out what's needed most: Quantity? Quality? Cost? Schedule? If you're going to customize your service for each client, then you need to know the relative importance of different types of service. Give the client what they value most.

You may be serving customers with conflicting interests. Emphasize that your role is to help the whole organization, and help each customer see the broader perspective. You may want to sit the different customers down with you to discuss the conflicts. What you don't want to do is deceive them by appearing to try to satisfy both clients without informing them of the conflict, under the assumption that they may never find out. If they do find out, not only is your reputation shot with those clients but also, through word of mouth, your reputation is damaged with other clients, too.

Treat add-ons as special requests or separate projects. Don't just take on additional work as a favor to the client. This is likely to encourage further requests. Clarify what's being asked of you, then explain how you can address it, and what effect it'll have on the schedule or the budget. Reach agreement and then commit to it.

Summarize all agreements before you part company. Provide follow-up confirmation. Depending on the number of people at the meeting and the nature of the meeting, you might consider having someone take notes. Those notes would then be written up, verified, and distributed to everyone present. If there were no official notes, then summarize the results in a follow-up note.

Complaints

How should you react to complaints, whether you feel they're justified or not. We've said that complaints should be encouraged. It's far better to receive a complaint first-hand rather than have it reach you, likely distorted, through rumor. And how can you fix your errors if your clients won't tell them to you? Here's some advice:

- Value complaints like gold, and share the wealth throughout I.S.
- Ask open questions
- Listen with body and soul
- Paraphrase frequently
- Solve whatever you possibly can immediately
- Thank your clients for their effort and involvement in I.S.

When you question a client about a process or a product, it's important to ask questions that can't be answered with a mere yes or no. Most people have difficulty raising awkward topics, and if you give a client an easy out, a question that only needs a yes or no, most clients will take it. Ask open questions.

Paraphrase frequently. Some books will advise you to say, "Let me see if I'm understanding you," or "Here's what it sounds to me that you're saying." When I'm in meetings, it's obvious that some people have just read these books because they sound programmed. "O.K., here's where I'm supposed to paraphrase to be sure I understand." Paraphrasing what someone else has said is a fine device for being sure you're understanding each other, but it must come naturally. When it sounds like a device, the speaker comes through as insincere.

Giving immediate attention to the complaints is obvious. If the complaint is justified, you want to rectify your error as quickly as possible. And some clients will respect you even more after you admit and resolve an error than if you'd never made the mistake in the first place.

Do thank the complainer. For most people, making a complaint is not much easier than accepting negative criticism. Reward the person who complained. You value the opportunity to make things right and the client should know it.

What if you don't believe the complaint is valid? Most likely, you will have an immediate negative reaction. If anyone else in I.S. has been involved, thank the client and say you'll look into the matter, then do so promptly. If the complaint appears to be unjustified, request a meeting with the client to discuss the situation. You need to determine where the difference in viewpoint has arisen. When you do find the source of the difference, either one of you will have recognized that you're wrong, or you should both understand that you're bringing different perspectives to the situation and should work to understand the other's perspective.

Hostility

It's getting worse. Complaints are delivered mildly, rationally. This time we have a client who is hostile. How do you react? Here are guidelines:

- Make the choice to stay calm
- Use active listening
- Keep your body in an open and relaxed position
- Show concern in your voice and face
- Be highly responsive to finding answers and quick solutions
- Keep the client informed frequently until the crisis is over

I say "Make the choice to stay calm" rather than simply "Stay calm," but it will be an effort. There is a conscious choice involved. When someone verbally attacks, the natural instinct in most people is to fight back. Use restraint.

The second, third and fourth items in the list all have to do with body language and non-verbal communication. Don't lean back and fold your arms in a closed position. Be alert and attentive. Show concern in your face, but it must be genuine. If somebody's this upset at you, there's probably a good reason behind it and you intend to understand it and respond to it. If your concern isn't real, you'll likely appear patronizing, and rightfully make your client all the angrier.

The last two items you'll do automatically because of your natural response to client concerns.

Resolving Client Indecision

There are again several guidelines that can be applied in helping your client make a decision about working with I.S. First, assess the client knowledge of technical options and their impact. Is it real or nod-knowledge? If it's only nod-knowledge, then you have some educating to do as you explain the options. It's important that your assessment be accurate, because otherwise you'll either be oversimplifying, possibly insulting the client, or you'll leave the client swirling in a sea of indecipherable words.

Understand that the more options you present to your client, the more confused and insecure he may become. Your head may be teeming with options, but keep a lid on them.

Outline three to five choices for your client. The client doesn't want to be told what he must do any more than he wants a menu of ten options to choose from. Be watchful for client understanding. Be sure client understanding puts all the pieces of your corporate puzzle together. The client's business is a piece. I.S. is a piece. All the pieces must fit together. The solution that's chosen must yield a completed puzzle after the work is finished.

Leave the decision with the client. There's nothing wrong with giving pros and cons of each option, as you see them, but the client should decide on the course to follow. He'll feel more in control and have a feeling of ownership. Nothing contributes more to client commitment than a feeling of ownership.

Use closed questions to edge the client off the fence. Under "Complaints," I urged you to ask open questions. Now, as you need a decision, you should phrase questions requiring definitive answers that will direct the client to a choice.

Lastly—something that repeatedly surfaces—show confidence, commitment, and caring.

Testing for Success

Before the client walks out the door, ask him if he's fully satisfied with the results of the meeting. If not, ask what would make him pleased with it. If he says he is happy with the results, then thank him for the opportunity to work with him.

Periodically, as you work with the client, use other techniques to test for success. Ask a client what he appreciates most that I.S. is doing. Ask what he'd like to see done differently. (Note that we're back to open questions.) If you get good suggestions for changes, make no on-the-spot promises. Thank the client for the feedback, then later get back to the client to explain either what changes have been implemented or why you decided against the changes suggested. But don't let the client think the suggestions went into a black hole. Be sure you get back to the client.

PERSONAL ACTION PLAN

Worksheet

MANAGING MOMENTS OF TRUTH

Specific ideas I can use on the job:

Specific actions I will take within 30 days:

Chapter 14

Creating a Service Team

*"No pessimist ever discovered the secrets of the stars, or sailed to
an uncharted land, or opened a new heaven to the human spirit."*
—Helen Keller

Selecting Team Members

The people who are on your I.S. service team is obviously crucial to
its success. Here are seven nonsequential steps for management to
follow after the commitment has been made to building superior service quality and being the #1 provider of choice.

1. What are the positions that will be needed in the new structure? How many of the current positions no longer need
   to exist in their present form? What are the restrictions as
   to personnel? Are you able to increase the size of I.S. to
   help provide superior service, or must you cut back people,
   "downsize," or "rightsize," your department while you re-
   structure?
2. Look carefully at present I.S. department members to analyze
   each person's strongest skills and interests. Is each one in the
   job that best suits their skills and interests? If not, how much
   juggling of positions can you do? What's your overall balance of technical and people skills? If you're shy on people

skills, how much can be learned by training, and to what degree do you need to bring in new people who already have the skills?

3. As you analyze the characteristics of your strongest performers, isolate traits that make them stand out. Are they needed qualities in the new system? If so, can those traits be taught to others? Should they be taught by professional trainers, or do those who have the traits also have the skills to teach them effectively?

4. For new employees, recruit whenever possible internally from existing employees, take referrals from successful employees to help bring you the talent you need. Look for team-oriented people who are interested in the type of work your organization does.

5. Those selected to be service team supervisors should be able to handle the "Jungle Cruise." Picture yourself at an amusement park on a jungle cruise or even better, imagine an actual jungle cruise. Wild animals jump out through the vines. Alligators surface right next to your boat, and you may have unthinkingly let your hand trail in the water. The service team supervisors must be able to handle the wild creatures of the business world in stride, staying on course, not panicking.

6. Use structured interview guides, panel interviews, tests, successful candidate profiles, assessment centers, and beef up interviewing skills. Let interviewed candidates and present workforce know that they'll be part of a winning team. Build enthusiasm and optimism by setting an example, not by browbeating it into them.

7. Take a little longer, be picky, careful and calculated. These are important decisions and the urge to begin the process will be strong. Having patience at the outset, making sure the right players are assembled, will be well worth the time it takes.

Preparing Service Providers

Train, train, train, and then train some more. Those aren't lyrics to a Johnny Cash song; it's a practice to follow. In these days of heavy personnel cutbacks, training is often one of the first areas to be cut. Yet at the same time, CEOs and management gurus are telling us that training is essential and must be increased if we are to remain competitive. Look at successful service organizations like Stew Leonards. They provide intensive training. Superior service doesn't just happen.

I.S. must come down firmly in the pro-training camp. Our staff must be comfortable and confident in their work. We can't afford to have them learn on the job. They must grow on the job, but the basic processes and facts should be known before any staff member meets with a client. We're one of the few areas of the company that influences every other area. Our services are essential to the health and growth of the entire organization. Therefore, our people must be at the top of their skills. We can't be satisfied with "smile and dial" telephone service reps. We're knowledgeable, personable, and work face-to-face with the entire company.

Make orientation for new hires a high-impact session. Involve present staff. As you present orientations for new hires, it would be helpful for existing staff to go through the session, too. After all, I.S. has changed a good deal since they had an orientation.

Both in the orientation and then while they're on the job, help your staff to know their clients and to know the business. Provide materials and tools for them to use.

Listen to service stories. Join professional organizations that stress service and training. Two of the largest are the American Society for Training & Development (ASTD) and the American Society for Quality Control (ASQC). Read their literature. Attend conferences and seminars, looking for emerging trends, changing standards, new ways to motivate and reward. Most industry-specific conferences have tracks devoted to service and quality. Never stop seeking ways for I.S. to improve.

Motivating the Staff

The emotional labor involved with client service is enormous. That's why motivation must be more than a shot in the arm of "feel good." You need a significant, well-supported motivation effort. It may include the following:

- *Recognition programs.* These usually take the form of awards and incentives, as discussed in Chapter 12.
- *Solid base pay.* These are important professionals and the pay must support that view.

■ *Career paths.* Establish a progression of jobs to get to the top of I.S. Let the staff know that skills they're learning will be especially important if they eventually leave I.S. Establish technical career paths for people who want to remain harnessed to the technology. You may not be able to afford as many of these people as before, but those you have will be invaluable. They also should know where their work can lead. You may want to require a minimum tour of duty as a primary service provider for anyone who aspires to a management position.

■ *Respect.* Management and fellow staff members must recognize the importance of service providers and act accordingly.

If the proper attitudes and values are instilled in the staff, there's no need to keep reminding people.

Setting Standards of Service

Through a careful analysis of Moments of Truth, you have arrived at a "success percentage" that is acceptable for each phase of the service process. This is not a figure that everyone knows, because everyone is trying for 100% (or better) satisfaction consistently. The acceptable rate is for management to use as they plan their resources and set priorities for action.

Standards of service should be:

■ Client generated
■ Expressed in terms of the client
■ Precise and measurable
■ Simple and clearly understood

I.S. should not need to rely on slogans. When you visit corporate America today, you see slogans plastering the walls. "Time is Money, Let's All Save," "We're All Rowing in the Same Direction," "Quality is #1." I think all these slogans are unnecessary and may be insulting. Slogans tend to be short-lived. They're the theme of the month. If the proper attitudes and values are instilled in the staff, there's no need to keep reminding people. Little kids need constant reminders; professionals don't.

PERSONAL ACTION PLAN

Worksheet

CREATING A SERVICE TEAM

Specific ideas I can use on the job:

Specific actions I will take within 30 days:

Chapter 15

Measuring Your Service

"Belief in experts' infallibility is one of the least likely to succeed strategies in the new business world."
—*Howard Stevenson and William A. Sahlman*

The Yardstick

This chapter will provide sample forms to help you measure the quality of your service. Feel free to make copies of the forms, or to adapt them so that the forms better fit your needs. However, as before, please give credit to Ouellette & Associates Consulting, Inc. as the source of the form.

Figure 15-1. The Client Service Yardstick

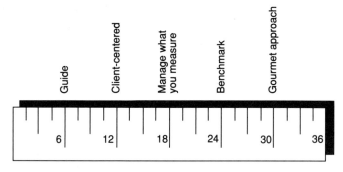

This Client Service Yardstick lets you know if you're "going the extra yard" beyond a typical service organization. If you publish a guide that describes your services to the client community, you've moved ahead six inches. Notice that this is not a guide of rules for internal behavior. There always needs to be a policy manual, but not a "proper behavior for good service" manual. This would be much like the slogans on the walls—artificial stimulants. The standards you're following will be stated in the guide for clients, and that should be sufficient for the staff, too.

You've progressed by a foot if your organization is clearly client-centered. Not technology-centered or I.S. staff-centered. You're looking for the best solution for the client and the entire company, even if it may not be computer-based.

If you "manage what you measure," you're halfway there. Too often, a department will have techniques for measuring their work, but are unable to follow up because they:

- Are not measuring the right things, or
- Don't know how to interpret the results, or
- Don't act upon the results because they don't want to accept the challenge, to make the effort.

Measurement should be an integral part of your standard procedures, and tools for measurement shouldn't just be grabbed off a shelf or out of a book, even this one. They should be carefully crafted to measure exactly what you need. And the tools should be created by people trained and experienced in creating targeted, unbiased surveys, questions and forms.

If you've gone beyond all other service programs you've seen, if you're offering unparalleled service with unique features that your clients rave about, then you've found a gourmet approach and have likely taken service as far as you can. But that's only for now. Times change, needs change, and you must be alert to new trends and be able to determine if a trend is a passing fad or a significant improvement.

Giving Credit

The personal touch is appreciated both by your staff and your clients. Identify the individuals who provide service. If it's design

Figure 15-2. Identification Tag

> The technician responsible for work performed on this system is:
> ### Sam Jones
> ### Ext. 331
> Please feel free to call if you have any questions.

or development of an application, give credit in the documentation. If it's writing the documentation, give credit in the front of the manual. If it's repair work on a system, you might affix a small plaque on the back of the same, something like the Identification Tag in Figure 15-2. Giving the name of a specific person to call helps humanize the repair process. It implies that a relationship exists.

The Report Card

Clients see your concern for good service when you provide a simple evaluation form after a service is provided. Figure 15-3 gives you a sample.

Figure 15-3. Immediate Evaluation Form

Your opinion in regard to the work completed is valued. Please complete the following information and return to:
John Doe Ext. 234

	GOOD	AVERAGE		FAIR	N/A
The person handling your request was:	5	4	3	2	1	
Technically knowledgeable	❑	❑	❑	❑	❑	❑
Attentive	❑	❑	❑	❑	❑	❑
Informative	❑	❑	❑	❑	❑	❑
Showing a sense of urgency	❑	❑	❑	❑	❑	❑
Courteous and helpful	❑	❑	❑	❑	❑	❑
Was job performed correctly in your opinion?	❑	❑	❑	❑	❑	❑
Did I.S. adhere to requested schedule?	❑	❑	❑	❑	❑	❑
Was clean-up performed after job completion?	❑	❑	❑	❑	❑	❑
Was the quality of work up to your expectations?	❑	❑	❑	❑	❑	❑

Additional comments:_____

Figure 15-4. Card for Evaluation

YOUR OPINION COUNTS

Information Services is requesting your assistance to help us determine the effectiveness of the services being provided by the I.S. organization. Please take just a few moments to fill out the accompanying survey to let us know how well our service(s) met your expectations. The information obtained from your input will be utilized to pinpoint areas requiring immediate attention, and assist us in implementing action plans to strengthen and improve our service to all clients. The I.S. organization is committed to providing you with quality, efficient and effective services. We sincerely want your feedback and thank you for taking the time to help us.

Jack Smith

(Fold on line and staple at bottom to return)

— —

Return to: John Doe
I.S. Manager
1400 Main Street
Anywhere, IL 60006

A convenient way to provide such a form is on a card, folded once, so that the survey is inside. Figure 15-4 shows how such a card might be designed.

Everyday Services

The "Your Opinion Counts" paragraph is generic enough to serve for either a brief card or a more elaborate survey. Figure 15-5 gives you a sample client survey about basic "everyday" services. The first part, a listing of I.S. service functions, both lets you know how often the service is used and the quality of the service provided. The next section deals with performance behaviors, including problem-solving. The final section of the survey asks clients which I.S. services are most important to them.

SURVEY OF BASIC SERVICES

For each I.S. service listed below, please indicate if you have or have not used the service within the past four months.

If you have used the service, please tell us your overall level of satisfaction, keeping in mind functionality, reliability and quality.

Figure 15-5. Survey of Basic Services

5 = Very satisfied
4 = Satisfied
3 = Neither satisfied or dissatisfied
2 = Dissatisfied
1 = Very dissatisfied

Function	Used service in last 4 months		5	4	3	2	1
	No	Yes					
Install/Move Desktop Computing Equipment							
■ Relocate or install any type of stand alone ADPE such as PCs, printers, and terminals.	❏	❏	❏	❏	❏	❏	❏
Repair/Maintain Desktop Computing Equipment							
■ Repair/maintain desktop systems such as PCs	❏	❏	❏	❏	❏	❏	❏
■ Upgrade H/W or S/W	❏	❏	❏	❏	❏	❏	❏
Telephone							
■ General use	❏	❏	❏	❏	❏	❏	❏
■ Move/add telephone	❏	❏	❏	❏	❏	❏	❏
■ Assign telephone number	❏	❏	❏	❏	❏	❏	❏
■ Telephone repairs	❏	❏	❏	❏	❏	❏	❏
Data Communications							
■ General use	❏	❏	❏	❏	❏	❏	❏
■ LAN installation	❏	❏	❏	❏	❏	❏	❏
■ Relocate/repair modems, data communications equipment	❏	❏	❏	❏	❏	❏	❏
■ Telephone repairs	❏	❏	❏	❏	❏	❏	❏

Figure 15-5.   Survey of Basic Services *(continued)*

Voice Mail System
- General use   ❐ ❐ ❐ ❐ ❐ ❐ ❐
- Features   ❐ ❐ ❐ ❐ ❐ ❐ ❐

Function **Mainframe Computing**	Used service in last 4 months No	Yes	5	4	3	2	1
Obtain computer account	❐	❐	❐	❐	❐	❐	❐
Application support	❐	❐	❐	❐	❐	❐	❐
Printing	❐	❐	❐	❐	❐	❐	❐
E-Mail	❐	❐	❐	❐	❐	❐	❐
Word processing	❐	❐	❐	❐	❐	❐	❐

This portion of the survey addresses the problem reporting and work request process. The purpose of this section is to determine how well we handled the initial request for service/help. Please indicate your overall level of satisfaction for each item.

Problem Reporting/Work Request

I.S. Support Desk Staff	Good 5	4	Average 3	2	Fair 1	N/A 0
1. Answered the phone promptly?	❐	❐	❐	❐	❐	❐
2. Was courteous?	❐	❐	❐	❐	❐	❐
3. Was attentive?	❐	❐	❐	❐	❐	❐
4. Was informative?	❐	❐	❐	❐	❐	❐
5. Was knowledgeable?	❐	❐	❐	❐	❐	❐
6. How effective was voice mail in helping solve your problem if you were unable to get through to Support Desk staff?	❐	❐	❐	❐	❐	❐
7. Were you able to obtain repair status updates?	❐	❐	❐	❐	❐	❐
8. Did you receive confirmation regarding your request?	❐	❐	❐	❐	❐	❐

Problem Resolution/Work Request Completion

	Good		Average		Fair	N/A
How well did we resolve problem or perform this work?	**5**	**4**	**3**	**2**	**1**	**0**
9. How do you rate I.S.'s response to your request?	❒	❒	❒	❒	❒	❒
10. Was the person handling your request:						
■ Technically knowledgeable?	❒	❒	❒	❒	❒	❒
■ Attentive?	❒	❒	❒	❒	❒	❒
■ Informative?	❒	❒	❒	❒	❒	❒
■ Show a sense of urgency?	❒	❒	❒	❒	❒	❒
■ Courteous, helpful?	❒	❒	❒	❒	❒	❒
11. Was job performed correctly in your opinion?	❒	❒	❒	❒	❒	❒
12. Did I.S. adhere to requested schedule?	❒	❒	❒	❒	❒	❒
13. Was follow through performed after job completion?	❒	❒	❒	❒	❒	❒
14. Was the quality of work up to your expectations?	❒	❒	❒	❒	❒	❒
15. Was procurement of systems/ components timely?	❒	❒	❒	❒	❒	❒
16. Was paperwork covering your work request adequate?	❒	❒	❒	❒	❒	❒
17. Did you receive follow-up information from I.S. pertaining to your work order?	❒	❒	❒	❒	❒	❒
18. Were you able to obtain follow-up information on your work order from I.S.?	❒	❒	❒	❒	❒	❒
19. Did you receive explanations of the problem?	❒	❒	❒	❒	❒	❒
20. Was work order completed without your intervention?	❒	❒	❒	❒	❒	❒
21. Was work performed to your satisfaction?	❒	❒	❒	❒	❒	❒
22. Were you satisfied with the overall performance of the various I.S. functions involved with processing your work order?	❒	❒	❒	❒	❒	❒

Figure 15-5.   Survey of Basic Services *(continued)*

Indicate three most important things to improve. Circle only **three** responses.
1. Response time to complete
2. Doing the job correctly
3. Adhering to schedule
4. Coordination of I.S. functions
5. Helpful personnel
6. Knowledgeable personnel
7. Equipment reliability
8. Equipment quality
9. Getting repair status updates
10. Increase uptime
11. Other: Please specify

---

12. Nothing to improve

Please print name clearly if you would like a response to items identified in this survey.
Thank you for your help. _____
                                        Name   **Extension**

This survey may look complex but is quick and easy to fill out. Most clients will recognize that you're concerned about your service quality and not feel that the survey is an imposition. I suggest that you circulate such a survey at the time you're planning your changes to improve service. After that, giving the survey once a year (at the most) should suffice, depending on changes implemented and turn-over either on the I.S. staff or in your client base.

Measurement Options

We've just taken a look at several specific ways you can measure I.S. service. Now let's take a look at a variety of ways measurement can be accomplished. You'll recognize some carryover from Chapter 8, when we looked at gathering information about your clients.

Each department must decide what's the most effective means of measurement. You must do enough measuring so that you have a solid statistical or factual base for how you rate the parts of your service, but you can't be measuring so often that it becomes an end in itself or an irritant to I.S. clients or IPPs.

Upper management needs to be impressed by the "new" I.S. department. Word of mouth may wind up being the most important factor, but whatever publicity you generate about your successes is also important. Distributing the results of your surveys and other forms of measurement provide the solid backbone to word-of-mouth and self-generated promotion. Too often, I.S. lacks enough measurement for valid results, and when the budget cuts come, we can't prove the impact our service has on our clients. The potential results are clear.

Measurement takes two basic forms: internal and external. External quality measurements include:

- Periodic client surveys
- Independent surveys of competition
- Post-installation surveys
- Records of client service cancellation
- Client query and complaint data analysis
- Client panels
- Client focus groups
- User groups

This is not an all-inclusive list, but does include the most commonly used methods. In order to helpfully tabulate client queries and complaints, it's necessary for them to have a structure. Many activities that may initially seem unmeasurable are only so because no one has stopped to think about their inherent parts and to provide structure to the process.

A client panel is a general discussion among the group of clients. A client focus group is different because the intent is to address one or more specific issues. There's greater structure to a focus group. A user group is a support group of people who all use the same application or the same hardware. A user group could form around SAS or around laptop computers. Therefore, their surveys, panels, or focus groups would, of necessity, focus on that particular application and the service relating to it.

Internal quality measurements include:

- Employee roles
- Scheduled roundtable discussions
- Extensive quality tests to achieve continuous improvements of products, procedures, and client services

Employee roles refers to how the employees use the equipment or software that's a daily part of their work. What is an effective means to measure their efficiency with their tools?

Downtime is a standard manufacturing measure. However, don't assume something is worthwhile just because it's been in use.

By "extensive quality tests," I simply mean that a quality test is not a one-time event. You're consistently monitoring for ongoing progress according to a schedule and an organized methodology for improvement.

> *Whatever form of benchmarking you use, it must yield quantifiable results that can demonstrate your progress to the rest of your organization.*

Benchmarking

One of the current fad words is "benchmarking," but it's used in several different ways, so when you hear it you've got to place it in its proper context. Either internal or external measures may be used in benchmarking.

"Benchmark" can mean measuring yourself against some external source. It can mean keeping close tabs on the competition and evaluating them against your capabilities. It can mean measuring yourself against a goal.

The "external source" is likely to be either the I.S. program in a company that's an acknowledged leader and innovator in I.S., or the I.S. groups from companies similar to yours. To measure yourself against either, you need to have the intelligence sources to keep close tabs on your rivals. That doesn't imply anything sneaky, but it does require a formal plan for how to gain such information. That type of business intelligence is beyond the scope of this book, but is often found in the general benchmarking literature, and one method of designing a program is detailed in Ruth Stanat's book, *The Intelligent Corporation* (AMACOM, 1990).

The easier form of benchmarking is a set goal for your group. It's a measure of progress from the current state to one you hope to attain, with both time frames and measurable changes included. Whatever form of benchmarking you use, it must yield quantifiable results that can demonstrate your progress to the rest of your organization.

PERSONAL ACTION PLAN

Worksheet

MEASURING YOUR SERVICE

Specific ideas I can use on the job:

Specific actions I will take within 30 days:

Chapter 16

Action Steps
to Better Service

"Even if you're on the right track, you'll get run over if you just sit there."

—*Will Rogers*

Taking Enough Action

If you've read the first fifteen chapters, you're definitely serious about this. So are a lot of other people. Next is the hardest step to take and that's action. That means more than doing "something"; it means doing "enough." The trend these days is not to make incremental changes but to evaluate your entire service system and then make a radical transformation.

As I've been writing this, General Motors has been in the news because Robert Stempel has stepped down as Chairman. The *Boston Globe* of October 28, 1992, published a comment from Thomas Hout of The Boston Consulting Group that bears upon the need for enough action. "GM has been seminared to death on classic Japanese mar-

> **Taking action means more than doing something; it means doing enough of the right thing.**

keting techniques—things like just-in-time production and fast-cycle engineering. They've overlearned. It's like going through the third grade five times. Now they need to show the guts to actually do some of this stuff."

Recall those people you knew who you thought of as professional students. They'd always be going for one more degree. In part, their motivation was a love of the academic life, a love of studying and learning. To implement service quality you must know when you've heard and read enough, when you're in danger of being "seminared to death." Then you've got to act.

There's no easy way to calculate how much action is enough. It's a measure of how far you have to go to get where you want to be.

A Service Model

This book has had numerous lists of things to do and to think about. What we're trying to do is present a complete model for action in a way that's easy to learn. In no way do we imply that because we're reducing complex behaviors to simple lists that the actions are easy to implement. We're discussing a full paradigm shift from the way most I.S. departments have operated in the past, and any change of that magnitude involves pain.

This is not easy to do, but it's essential to do. Some people just go through the motions. Following the actions is much easier than changing the thought patterns. That's why this is a paradigm shift, because it requires a change not just in people's conscious reactions, but also in people's instinctive reactions.

Next I'd like to give you the service model we follow at Ouellette & Associates. That doesn't mean it's posted on the walls, or that we get together every day at 9 A.M. and recite it in unison. It's simply a simplified and clever (and more memorable because it's simplified and clever) guide to the right thoughts and behavior.

Figure 16-1. O&A Service Model

Sensitivity
Be sensitive to your clients' needs and your Moments of Truth as service opportunities. Make them payoff.

Empathize
Put yourself in your clients' shoes. Try to feel what they are feeling.

Respect
Always respect your clients regardless of personal differences, dislikes or personality styles.

Vow
Vow your commitment to 100% client satisfaction in attitude, principles and practice.

Instant
Respond instantly to client requests, complaints or suggestions.

Care
Show your clients that you really care about helping them. Non-verbally, verbally and in writing. Always let them know you care.

Enthusiasm
Be optimistic, show genuine commitment to serve during each client interaction.

Service Action Checklist

Here are a variety of fairly immediate actions you can take. They won't upset the apple cart, but they will alert people that something's afoot. They're just suggestions. Add to the list or change items if they'll then be more appropriate for you. The important point is to do something now. Don't put off beginning.

The Commitment to Action Checklist in Figure 16-2 is in three parts, things to be completed within the next forty-eight hours, within the next week, and within the next month. It's designed to assure that you're learning more about service and about your clients and are instituting immediate measures to improve service in small ways. These small moves will be paving the way for the larger announcement about the total staff commitment to being the service provider of choice.

COMMITMENT TO ACTION CHECKLIST

The following "call to action" are suggestions for immediately increasing your service and effectiveness with your clients. We wish you well and would appreciate hearing from you as you complete your checklist.

Figure 16-2. Commitment to Action

Action Item	**Completion Date**

Within the next 48 hours:

1. Decide that the most important thing you can focus on is superior client service. _____

2. Call three clients, ask them how you can provide better service, then sit back and listen. _____

3. Send three handwritten thank you notes to clients for working with you. _____

4. Be sure every client commitment is likely to be kept, and gives you room to exceed expectations. _____

5. Ask one colleague a day "what have you done for the client today?" _____

6. Start a 5 P.M. ritual of writing out your plans to provide superior client service for the next day. _____

Within the next week:

1. Mention the importance of delivering superior client service to five colleagues. _____

2. Ask your clients what areas of your work/ organization they'd like to be better informed about. _____

3. Meet individually with your top five clients and find out what their top five business challenges are in the next year and then the next three years. _____

4. Send three handwritten notes to colleagues who've helped you provide superior service to your clients. _____

5. Institute a policy in your organization for making sure all clients who visit your work area are introduced personally to any of our staff they may have contact with. _____

6. Set up a lunch meeting or coffee break with your best client and best potential client just to talk. _____

Figure 16-2. Commitment to Action *(continued)*

Action Item   **Completion Date**

Within the next month:

1. Put together a plan to help your clients
   with their business challenges you just
   discovered.   _____

2. Compile a list of your clients birthdays
   and send a card or take them to lunch on
   that day.   _____

3. Circulate at least three articles on superior
   client service.   _____

4. Identify one way to enhance the quality
   of the service you provide your five largest
   clients and do them.   _____

5. Arrange to sit in on your clients staff
   meetings, business meetings, or when
   they are meeting with their clients
   and learn about their world and business.   _____

6. Ask five clients their impressions of how
   they're handled over the telephone when
   calling your office.   _____

7. Ask everyone in your organization
   what courses, conferences, reading
   materials, etc. will help you improve your
   client service.   _____

8. Find one foolish rule in your organization
   that prohibits you from delivering superior
   client service and eliminate it.   _____

9. Read one leading book or article on
   providing superior client service.   _____

10. Subscribe to at least one of your clients'
    business journals or periodicals.   _____

11. Call yourself to evaluate the department
    response.   _____

PERSONAL ACTION PLAN

Worksheet

ACTION STEPS TO BETTER SERVICE

Specific ideas I can use on the job:

Specific actions I will take within 30 days:

Personal Action Plan Revisited

The Service Action Checklist can apply, with small variations, to just about anyone. You need a guide to action that's tailored to your needs. As you've been reading, I hope you've been underlining or making notes in the margin and filling in the individual Personal Action Plan Worksheets at the end of each chapter. Now is the time to bring all those notes and highlights together.

Following are fresh sheets for your total Personal Action Plan. We include two pages for "Specific ideas I can use on the job," and two pages for "Specific actions I will take within 30 days." Review the Worksheets you've completed. It may be easiest for you to make a copy of each Worksheet so you can review them all together. Add or remove items based on reading in subsequent chapters and ideas you've had about your work while you were reading.

PERSONAL ACTION PLAN

Worksheet

Specific ideas I can use on the job:

PERSONAL ACTION PLAN
(Page 2)

Specific ideas I can use on the job:

PERSONAL ACTION PLAN
(Page 3)

Specific actions I will take within 30 days:

PERSONAL ACTION PLAN
(Page 4)

Specific actions I will take within 30 days:

Summary of Service Action Plan

Now that you're so totally immersed in detail and excited by the prospects that your head is swimming, it's time to zero in on what's really most important to you. On the following page, list the ten top priority steps you commit to take in the next 30 days to strengthen your service effectiveness with your clients. Armed with this limited list, and the four pages of Personal Action Plan items, you're ready to begin. Go to it, and good luck.

SUMMARY OF SERVICE
ACTION PLAN

1.

2.

3.

4.

5.

6.

7.

8.

9.

10.